MEMORIES OF EVIL

MEMORIES OF EVIL

"THE ONLY THING WE LEARN FROM HISTORY
IS THAT WE NEVER LEARN ANYTHING FROM HISTORY."

*Memoir of a World War II childhood,
written in the fervent hope, perhaps naive,
that Hegel's dictum is wrong.*

PETER KUBICEK

Design and composition: David G. Shaw, Belm Design
Cover design by Herbert Koch.

Produced in the United States of America

Kubicek, Peter
Memories of Evil
1. Memoir   2. The Holocaust
3. World War II   4. History of Slovakia
Version 1.0 – February 2006
Library of Congress Control Number: 2006921089

Author's Note

This is an expanded version of a memoir I published in 2006 under the title *1000:1 ODDS*.

A memoir of this type is emotionally very difficult to write. You are forced to dredge up, fragment by fragment, painful, long-buried memories which you had previously hoped to forget. While the process caused me untold sleepless nights, ultimately the writing process proved to be a real catharsis. As I came closer to the end of my story I could not wait to write *Finis* and thereby get this heavy load off my chest. But subsequently I received so many interesting comments and questions that I came to the realization that I could have and should have said more. After a period of reflection I went back to my manuscript and gradually wrote a number of additions. I also added a few more personal photographs, which luckily had been saved by my father and mother, since I saw that readers were fascinated by these ancient-looking glimpses of the past. This current book is the result.

I was also motivated by the fact that we Holocaust survivors are a dying breed: within a couple of decades we will be extinct. It is to me of great importance that the testimony we leave behind be authentic, truthful and historically accurate. This sentiment would seem to be obvious, but unfortunately it is not. I have been a careful student of the Holocaust for great many years. The vast amount of misinformation I have come across is simply staggering. The errors I have found ranged from minor to major, to malicious. I have come across fake memoirs, fake films, fake theses and private viewpoints masquerading as fact. With the information explosion on the internet, misinformation thrives and spreads and does untold damage to the cause of truth about the Holocaust. I have been very active in the effort to debunk the fake and the phony whenever I could, wherever I found it.

This memoir is but a small tessera in the complex mosaic of the inexpressible evil we call the Holocaust. May my modest contribution serve as my epigraph.

Table of Contents

Prologue

I have a fond memory of a lovely French movie called "The Two of Us" about a small boy who is hidden throughout the Second World War with a peasant couple in the countryside. His parents have impressed on his memory that he must never, under any circumstances, admit to being a Jew. The movie begins with a voice-over by the boy saying, "When the war started I was only eight years old, but I was already a Jew."

What a revealing sentence! The boy considers being a Jew such a heavy, grown-up burden that it should not be placed upon the shoulders of a mere child. It reminded me of when I was about his age, at the start of World War II, and of a later time when I was fourteen years old and found myself in a concentration camp, desperately alone, miserable, terrified, feeling like a grain of sand being tossed around by a vicious, violent ocean. What were my chances of survival?

When my twin daughters, Katia and Mia, were fourteen years old, I looked upon them as these two delicate buds needing so much nurture and protection and I thought back to when I was their age and I marveled once again how it was that I had survived. I decided then to write a short memoir, meant strictly for my daughters, describing for them the events surrounding my fifteenth birthday, one that I spent in a concentration camp, and to present it to them on their fifteenth birthday.

I wrote that memoir in 1982-1983. This present memoir expands the one for my daughters. It goes back to my childhood before the War and continues to the day I arrived in the United States and embarked upon my new life.

I grew up in the town of Trenčín, in the former Czechoslovakia, now the Slovak Republic. Even small towns in Europe are frequently quite old. Owing to its strategic location between a wide river, backed by steep hills, the settlement of Trenčín started in the second century C.E., when the Roman army established a fortified camp there. Slav tribes inhabited the town beginning in the fifth century. For hundreds of years it was under Hungarian rule during which time it became an important county seat, with a concentration of various administrative offices. So it remained, even after the creation of Czechoslovakia in 1918.

When I was a child, the town had some 18,000 inhabitants. Jews, who made their appearance in Trenčín during the 16th century, numbered about 2,000. This may seem a puny town by American standards, but within the small country of Slovakia it was, and remains, quite substantial. Many still smaller towns and villages surrounded it and they looked to Trenčín for essential services. If you had business at a government office, or at a court, you had to go to Trenčín. The same was true for a hospital, a middle school, a doctor, a lawyer, or even a store with a better selection of goods.

In the town's central square, at the most prominent location, was situated "Drogeria Kubiček," my father's store. It was like a miniature department store. Here you could find any article that a drug store carried, as well as such disparate goods as luggage and leather items, cameras, or sports equipment. To buy a gift, have film developed, even have a tennis racquet restrung, you would come to Drogeria Kubiček. Upon entering the store, you would see my grandfather at the cash register and my mother behind a counter. My mother loved working in the store, much preferring it to running the household. For the latter she had a maid and a cook, and a governess for me. This was not necessarily a reflection of great wealth, it was just the way the middle, or upper- middle class lived.

Here I am at age 3 or 4, in the typical sailor's suit that every little boy of good family had to own.

With my grandfather Adolf Kubicek, at our store's cash register

With my grandfather Josef Kobler, in front of a nearby store.
The sign above our heads says "Milk for sale."

Both of my grandfathers died in the 1930's of natural causes and were thus spared the torture and agonizing death that would no doubt have awaited them had they lived into the 1940's.

And here, looking very much older, at the age of 6 or 7

This photo was taken in the outdoor café of the town park. On pleasant Sunday afternoons, my parents would take me for a walk in the park which always ended at the café. Here my standard treat was an open-face sandwich. The sandwiches were served cut into triangles, each small piece speared by a toothpick. This enabled a party to order two or three sandwiches and easily share them. This also appealed to my sense of fastidiousness in that I could pick up each piece without my fingers coming into contact with whatever sticky food covered it. My favorite accompanying drink was raspberry syrup mixed with sparkling water. This was served with a straw, through which I alternately sipped and blew bubbles into the drink. My mother, who always tried to instill good manners in me, pretended to be aghast at my behavior.

5

The town park was an agreeable and popular spot for the local inhabitants. I was familiar with it since my early childhood when my governess would take me there to its playground. Here we could always find little friends with whom I could play, while my governess could sit on a bench and gossip with her colleagues. Of course, a few years later, once the anti-Semitic laws were promulgated, Jews were prohibited from entering any public venue and our Sundays in the park were over.

Should you have wanted to find me in the store, the section to look for me was the toy department in the back, a place of eternal fascination to a child like me. Some times my father would let me borrow a toy or game, on condition that I return it at the end of the day, in the same pristine condition as I had found it. A day or two sometimes stretched the return policy, but my father could always count on me to return the borrowed item in perfect, salable condition.

At age 8 with my mother

My parents participated in the cultural and social life of the town. The cultural selection was hardly extensive, but my parents simply attended every musical or theatre performance that came through town, presented by touring professional or amateur groups. Formal balls and events of society would take place in the ballroom of the Hotel Tatra, to this day the best hotel in town. The Trenčín soccer stadium and its soccer team drew large crowds for intense matches against rival teams from other towns.

My parents kept a kosher home, as did most Jews of the region. My paternal grandparents lived with us. After their deaths the standards of *kashrut* relaxed. Sunday was the traditional day off for the household help. On that day we traditionally ate a cold dinner, generally cold cuts and salads. On occasion we ate ham, which my mother loved, but it was served on paper plates, so that our dishes would remain impeccably kosher. With my father a pillar of our local, Conservative synagogue, I understood that I had to be discreet and keep mum about our ham dinners.

My parents attended synagogue services mainly on major holidays. I, however, was a boy soprano in the synagogue choir and so had to attend services every Saturday, as well as choir rehearsals. I have pleasant memories of that experience. The choir director was young; he kept teaching us new songs and made practice a lot of fun.

Zionism was an important part of our lives. My parents were both active in Zionist organizations (and remained so to the end of their days). Zionist meetings were held in our house; my parents contributed time and money to the cause. Our town had a very active *Hashomer Hatzair* Zionist organization, with a very good children's program that I eagerly attended from early childhood. We had weekly *slichot*, or meetings, at which we were lectured on Palestine and taught Hebrew songs, games and dances. We put on plays and musicals for the Jewish community. We

often went on hikes. My love of hiking, which remains undimin-
ished to this day, is attributable to that early experience.

At age 8 with my father

Memory works in mysterious ways. Like most people,
I do not remember my past in day-to-day detail. Some scenes,
however, remain imbedded in my memory in exquisite vividness
and I can see them in my mind's eye and describe them as if I
were looking at a snapshot. Here is one:

A few friends and I are walking home from a *slichah*. Someone suggests that we get something to eat; not just anything, but a *klobása*. This is a pork sausage, a great Slovak specialty and to us a forbidden, but alluring food. We pool our money and come up with, say, 1.75 Slovak crowns. One boy and I are nominated to make the dangerous purchase. Stealthily we enter a butcher shop and ask for a 1.75 crowns worth of *klobása*. "What kind?" asks the butcher, pointing to an array of his products. We ask for whichever we can get the most of for our money. He cuts off a hunk of the cheapest and greasiest sausage. We run out of the store with the cry, "We got it!" Our little group then scurries to an isolated spot where we carefully cut the sausage into equal pieces and consume them with glee. Oh, Adam, had you but known the paradisiacal taste of a Slovak *klobása* you would surely have spurned the proverbial forbidden apple!

In August, 1939, as the clouds of war were gathering over Europe, my father left for the World Zionist Congress in Geneva, Switzerland, as a delegate from Slovakia. While there, Germany attacked Poland and World War II broke out. My father's first reaction was to rush back home to us, but friends persuaded him that he could help us more if he stayed in Switzerland and tried to get us out of Czechoslovakia. He tried his best, but the Swiss blocked all his efforts to rescue us and denied us entry. After a few months, they even kicked my father out of their country.

My father moved on to Paris. With the German army approaching, he was forced to move further, to the south of France. From there he tried to enter Spain. That country's fascist government, however, did not allow in any refugees without a proper visa and visas were next to impossible to obtain. At one point of entry, though, my father came upon a heroic Portuguese consul, a man by the name of Aristides de Sousa Mendes, whose name should be celebrated as one of those rare righteous gentiles, who stamped his country's visa into any passport placed in front of him, waiving all fees. This allowed my father passage through Spain, into Portugal. Spain was ruled by Francisco Franco, a dictator who greatly admired Hitler and his ideas. Portugal's ruler, Antonio Salazar, was also a dictator, and, though not exactly eager to have his country overrun by refugees, he showed compassion to them once they arrived there. His compassion, though, had limits. Sousa Mendes was ultimately stripped of his authority and recalled to Portugal. When he criticized the government, and continued to defend his deeds on humanitarian and religious grounds, he was fired from his diplomatic post and eventually died in poverty.

My father arrived in Lisbon, a city full of frightened refugees, all of them seeking visas to countries in the Western Hemisphere, such as the United States, the various countries of South and Central America, Cuba, the Dominican Republic. The consulates of all these countries were besieged by refugees. They continually made the rounds of the consulates and then gathered in the coffeehouses, to exchange information and listen to the myriad circulating rumors. In recalling this tense period, my father always praised the great kindness of the Portuguese people.

After several months, the U.S. Consulate finally informed my father that his visa was granted. In March 1941, he was able to board a ship in Lisbon, the *Serpa Pinto*. After an odyssey of one year and seven months he arrived in New York City. He immediately continued with his efforts to obtain security for his family by obtaining U.S. visas for us, too. Sol Bloom, a local congressman and compassionate man, listened to my father's desperate entreaty to help him save us. He interceded with the State Department on our behalf. Miraculously, as it seemed to us, in September 1941, my mother, my maternal grandmother and I were invited to Budapest for an interview with the U.S. consul.

By that time, Czechoslovakia had ceased to exist. The Czech lands were annexed by Germany, renamed The Protectorate of Bohemia and Moravia, while Slovakia had become a quasi-independent Fascist state, proudly allied with Nazi Germany. It was now run by the *Hlinka Guard*, named after its founder, Andrej Hlinka, and patterned after the Nazi Storm Troopers. They had installed their own government, led by President Josef Tiso, a Catholic priest deeply involved in fascist politics. A virulent streak of anti-Semitism united the Slovak fascists with their German Nazi brethren.

The U.S., naturally, had no representation in Slovakia, hence the call to us from Budapest, the seat of the nearest U.S. consulate. Getting there was no easy matter. Arrangements were finally made that allowed us to board a sealed bus, together with about a dozen other lucky people, which took us to Budapest for the consular interview and then back. A few weeks later we were given the marvelous news that our U.S. visas were granted! However, travel from Slovakia to the United States was, at this point, extremely difficult. My father worked on obtaining passage for us on a ship from a French port, while my mother tried to get the necessary documents, permits and transit visas needed to get to France. Weeks passed and then came December 7, 1941, "a day that will live in infamy" for me and my family, as much as for all Americans. The Japanese attack on Pearl Harbor brought with it the end of all civilian travel across the Atlantic Ocean. My mother, my grandmother, and I were trapped.

At age 11 with my mother.

1940-1941: The Screws Tighten

At the start of 1940, during my father's odyssey, the Slovak government promulgated a series of anti-Semitic laws, designed to gradually choke off Jewish life. The major step was the *aryanization*, or expropriation of all Jewish businesses. These businesses were generally taken over by Slovak employees who were deemed to be good Party members. Since many of these were unable to run these business by themselves, they kept the former Jewish owners as their employees. In some instances, a feeling of guilt and some vestige of decency played a part here. My mother had been running our family business by herself since my father left. We had no great luck with our *arizator* (the aryanizer). Laci Breuer, a native German who lived in Slovakia, had been a long-time employee of ours. He started with us as a young trainee and was gradually promoted. Early on he even lived in our house. When his mother came to visit him, my parents welcomed her as a guest and she stayed in our house. Laci and I sometimes played together after store hours. I remember roughhousing with him in our backyard and riding on his shoulders.

When he took over our store, his first act was to fire my mother. At a later time, as the crisis deepened, a gentile Slovak, in an effort to help us, approached Laci with a request for some assistance to us and was told, "My political career would be jeopardized if it became known that I had helped Jews." By that time he was a prominent member of the Nazi party.

All Jews in Slovakia had to wear yellow stars. These were about five inches in size, made of cloth, and had to be sewn onto our outer garments, at chest height. We were subject to a curfew and not allowed on the streets after 6 pm. We were forbidden to walk on the main square and, as that was where my family lived, we had to move into an apartment on a back street. We were not allowed in places of public entertainment, such as movie houses, theaters, or restaurants. Notices appeared on entrances to public establishments, "Jews and dogs not allowed." What I missed most was the town swimming pool, where I had spent carefree summers. Jews were not allowed to own "luxury articles," such as automobiles, radios, cameras, jewelry, furs etc. The list went on and on. Sports equipment was on this list, too, and I was forced to give up my sled, my skis, my soccer ball, and my most prized possession of all, my red bicycle. My mother later recalled that I once came home crying, after I saw a boy on the street riding my bicycle.

While we lived in our second apartment, a local minor party functionary moved into an identical apartment, a floor below us. One day he came up to our floor, rang our doorbell, introduced himself to my mother as Mr. Masnik, and asked to see our apartment. Apparently deciding that our elegant living room furniture would look so much better in *his* empty living room, he simply arranged with the Party to "aryanize" the content of our living room. He came back a few days later with some of his henchmen and they emptied our living room of everything, including furniture, rugs, lamps, ashtrays, and the cabinets with all their contents. He then arranged all of it identically in his apartment.

Jewish children were no longer allowed to attend non-Jewish schools. Our town's Jewish elementary school originally had five grades, which the Jewish community now expanded by adding three more. The school's auditorium was converted into one large classroom for all three extra grades. I attended that extra classroom which had only one teacher who taught the three grades simultaneously and heroically managed to keep order and hold our interest.

During the summers of 1940 and 1941, we Jewish children of Trenčín spent most of our time out on the Váh, the wide river that flowed swiftly past the town. By this time, Jews were not allowed to congregate in groups, so we met in smaller units of no more than three or four and walked separately upriver, beyond the outskirts of the town. There we congregated on a large stretch of overgrown wilderness. That's where we spent our entire days. We picnicked and we swam. Often we went exploring a couple of miles upriver and then swam downstream with the current, exploring further wild terrain on either side.

An occasional occurrence, always eagerly anticipated, added much to our fun. It was signaled by someone yelling, *"Plte!"* — Rafts! — and pointing upstream. All of us would instantly jump up and look for the expected rafts as they languidly floated into our view. We now started running upstream and then plunged into the river and swam to meet the rafts. These were made of long, thick logs that were lashed together to form a large floating platform. It was lumber that was felled in the forests of distant mountains and was being conveyed for processing to lumber mills located a few hundred miles downstream. This was simply a cheap mode of transportation. Each raft was manned by two raftsmen who spent a couple of weeks guiding it to its destination. The raft was fitted with one long oar in front and one in the back. Generally, only one oarsman was needed to give an occasional tug on his oar to keep the raft on course. Both raftsmen became alert only when they passed between spans of a bridge, or on dangerous stretches of the river. So, while one man was on duty in the front, the other relaxed in the back where they had a lean-to in which they could take shelter and in which they slept. In front of it they generally had a fireplace going on which they cooked their meals.

A squealing bunch of us children quickly invaded the rafts. The raftsmen were amused by our presence and chatter, which must have afforded them a pleasant break in their unvarying routine. As we approached the inhabited part of the town, we said good-bye to our new friends and swam back to shore. We definitely did not want any of the townspeople to see us. For while we seemed like a carefree bunch of kids, we were also well aware that we had to watch our step at all times. The raftsmen did not know that we were Jews — after all we did not wear our obligatory yellow stars on our bathing suits — and had they known, I have no idea what their reaction would have been. It may have ranged from, "Who cares, I just see a bunch of kids having fun;" to, "Goddam stinking Jews, get off my raft!" Either scenario would have been entirely plausible, so we just did not take any unnecessary chances.

By the end of the afternoon we reunited at our gathering spot and from there dispersed in smaller groups back to town. The river had its dangers and it claimed a few victims every year. Notwithstanding the trepidation and worries of our parents, we all became excellent swimmers and never encountered any problem, neither from the river's swift currents and rocky sections, nor from any Slovaks. Most of the town's inhabitants were unfamiliar with this wilderness and the occasional fisherman or amorous couple that ventured there never bothered us.

Children are everlastingly adaptable. In spite of the difficult situation in which our community found itself, and the seemingly myriad onerous restrictions placed on our lives, we kids made the best of it, and I remember the summers of 1940 and 1941 as almost idyllic. All of us, adults as well as children, truly believed that our task was just to keep a low profile and outlast the war.

1942: The Year Of Ravage

In March, 1942, the Slovak government embarked with great determination and enthusiasm on the task of annihilating Slovak Jewry, a community of close to 90,000 people. The Slovaks were assured by Germany that the Germans would handle the actual killing; Slovakia needed only to round up the Jews and deport them. In return, the Slovaks would get to keep and distribute to their loyalists whatever Jewish property remained, an irresistible offer, too good to refuse.

As announced, the initial policy was that only young, able-bodied, unmarried Jews would be deported "to labor camps, in the East." Young couples without children soon followed these. Finally, the Slovak henchmen dropped all pretenses and proceeded to deport the young, the old and entire families. Frightened, we clung to the belief that the propaganda was true; that labor camps were to be our destination. We believed it because it sounded so logical. Jewish leadership disseminated advice on how to prepare for the camps: buy sturdy boots, pack warm clothing into durable luggage and backpacks. They issued checklists of useful items to take along. "And don't forget to pack some games for those long winter evenings" we were admonished. Wishful thinking and "logic" dictated our belief in this advice. Only much later did we learn that all these preparations were pointless.

Only so-called "economically important Jews" were exempt from deportation. These included employees of aryanized businesses who were still needed to run them. Physicians, though not allowed private practice, often managed to obtain employment in hospitals, and so were protected. Several additional categories of employment offered exemption and there was a mad scramble to obtain such coveted jobs, no matter how insignificant or menial.

Then there was *protekcia*, a form of protection. Jews had been fully integrated in Slovak life and many had non-Jewish friends who were now influential. Some of these had the decency to use their power to help Jews. There was also one quality that distinguished Slovaks from the Germans in that they were eminently bribable. For Jews who still had money a lot was possible. My mother had some money, friends in the non-Jewish community and influential friends within the Jewish community. For a time this kept us on the "exempt" list.

Among my mother's influential Jewish friends was the best friend of our family. He contributed immeasurably to our survival and remains greatly cherished in my memory. As a lieutenant in the Austro-Hungarian army during the First World War, my father developed a close friendship with another lieutenant named Adolf (Adko) Strassmann. After that war, they both settled in the same town, where they both started businesses and prospered. Each got married: Adko first, and he and his wife, Franzi, had a daughter, Ela, and a son, Paul (Palo). My father, Andor (Andrew) was next to marry and I was born exactly one year and two days after Paul. The Kubiček and Strassmann families remained so close that they practically functioned as one family unit. When my father left the country, Adko became, in effect, my surrogate father. A man of exceptional drive and ability, he had unsurpassed connections among the local Slovaks. This gave him influence to protect his extended family. Due to his help our names remained on the exempt list.

Last joint photograph of the Kubicek and Strassmann families, in 1939, at the swimming pool of a nearby spa.
From left to right: myself, Ela Strassmann, Adko Strassmann, Andor Kubicek, Ilka Kubicek, Cecilie Kobler (Ilka's mother), Paul and his mother Franzi Strassmann.

Reverse of preceding photograph, which became a postcard that I mailed to my uncle Fred. He had fled from Vienna in 1938, when the Germans occupied Austria, and escaped to Paris. He was known to his family as Fritz, but, long before the war, the Czechoslovak authorities had forced him to change this German name to the Czech Bedrich. Note that I am showing off my precocious knowledge of English. Under my signature is a P.S. by my father, in German, a cryptic reference to some collection of samples. This is some kind of private code between the two brothers-in-law.

One day, however, our luck ran out. A couple of *Hlinka* Guardsmen, the Slovak equivalent of the German Nazis, rang our doorbell and told us to prepare to go with them to the railroad station, for deportation to Žilina. Žilina is the name of the town in which a Slovak concentration camp had been founded; from there transports left for unknown "points East." My mother's protestation of her "economically important" designation had no effect, and she, my grandmother and I found ourselves on a train to Žilina, in our sturdy boots and with our backpacks and luggage. In the Žilina concentration camp guards herded us into a large room in what had been military barracks. It contained no beds or bunks; only loose straw on the floor. Here each family enclosed a portion of the floor with its luggage and arranged its living and sleeping space within this boundary.

Once or twice each week a transport of exactly 1,000 people left from Žilina in cattle cars. None of us knew that these were bound for extermination camps in Poland. Even in this Žilina camp a group of people were exempt from the final deportation. These included some who worked in the camp's administration, its building and maintenance crews, and people with *protekcia*. When our first "transport day" dawned, our family was moved into the "exempt" building, by virtue of our *protekcia*, a sign that Adko's good connections were working. For as soon as Adko found out that we had been "taken," he immediately started working on his Slovak connections to save us. As a preliminary, he managed to get us into the camp's exempt group. On our day of deportation, the transport for some reason did not add up to the requisite number of 1,000 people. Functionaries arrived in our "exempt" building and started calling out names of people who were to be added to the transport, their exemption notwithstanding. I am still haunted by the chilling scene of the desperate family of a friend of mine crying when their names were called. Their entreaties were, of course, to no avail.

We went through two such transport days, with their attendant tense wait in the "exempt" building, listening to the unavailing cries of the people being pulled and pushed out of it. After about ten days in the camp, during which daily arrivals kept swelling our ranks, we were miraculously granted release and returned to Trenčín. With the help of my mother's hidden reserve of cash, Adko Strassmann had worked his magic.

The deportations stopped abruptly in the latter part of 1942. Close to 60,000 people had been deported, the vast majority of them sent to their death. Of the remnant, several thousand were transferred and incarcerated in two Slovak forced-labor camps. There, in spite of harsh conditions, neither actual killings, nor deportations took place, and survival was possible.

These are the actual statistics:

• Population of Slovak Jews at the beginning of 1942: 89,500

• Deported in 1942: about 59,500

The remaining 30,000 Jews were divided among the following groups:

• Those who were "protected" or exempt, though without any property or civil rights: about 15,000

• Those who escaped (mainly to Hungary) and those in hiding: about 10,500

• Those in Slovak labor camps: about 4,500

By the end of 1942, most of my Jewish classmates and playmates were gone, as were most of my relatives: my cousins, uncles, and aunts. For almost all of them their life ended in the gas chambers. Some were sent to the Slovak labor camps. By the war's end, only a pitiful few of them actually survived the concentration camps.

My family and the Strassmanns were among the few Jews left in Trenčín. We were forced to move a second time, to even humbler quarters, in a working-class neighborhood, at the outskirts of town. The location did have a certain advantage though, in that here it was easier to disappear from public view and consciousness.

January 26, 1943 — my 13th birthday

This would have been the date of my *Bar Mitzvah*. A year before, Paul still celebrated his special day and, in accordance with our ancient tradition, was called to the Torah in the synagogue. But, due to all the restrictions on our life, his father would not risk having a party for Paul in their apartment. So, an uncle of his who lived in the outskirts of town offered his apartment for Paul's party. His classmates and friends were invited, as well as our teacher. In the middle of the party we suddenly heard a loud banging on the door, and shouts of the dreaded words, "Open up! Police!" Some neighbor had apparently called them to report that Jews were congregating here and the police came to investigate and to enforce the anti-Jewish laws. Our teacher reasoned with them and pointed out that only children were present, celebrating a birthday. The police relented and told us that no arrests would be made, providing we broke it up right away.

By 1943 my *Bar Mitzvah* was out of the question. The Jewish community of Trenčín had ceased to exist. Most of my classmates had been deported during the previous year and were by now dead.

To commemorate the *Bar Mitzvah* that could not be, my mother took me to a photographer and splurged by having this portrait made, as a memento for my father. From the inscription on the back of the photo, in a handwriting I do not recognize, I deduce that my mother managed to mail it to an acquaintance of my father's in Portugal, with the request to forward it to my father, without any identification as to its origin.

1943-1944: We Lie Low

This was a time of great shortages. We did not starve, however, thanks to my grandmother's prodigious feats in the kitchen. She invented meatless hamburgers, made from chopped vegetables and breadcrumbs; she made ersatz coffee from roasted chicory. Using scraps of fat and whatnot, following some arcane recipe, she made soap.

My mother, in particular, was bothered by the lack of the fine soap to which she had been accustomed when she had a great selection in our store. When her birthday approached I got an idea for a present that I thought may please her. I decided to confront Laci Breuer in our former store. Ignoring the regulation prohibiting Jews from entering the main square, I walked into the store and told Laci about my mother's birthday and asked him for a couple of pieces of good soap for her. He pulled a face, but did come up with two cakes of fine prewar soap from a hiding place under a counter. He charged me the full retail price and gave me to understand that he did not want to see me in "his" store again.

My duty at this time was to gather fuel for our wood-burning stove in the kitchen and to keep the fire going. I collected wood, mostly scraps of lumber, which we stored in a little shed we had the use of, about a block away. There I chopped wood boards into kindling and carried a daily pile to our apartment house, up one staircase, and into our kitchen. Upon arising each morning, I first lit the fire, then got myself ready for the day in the bathroom and then rushed back to the fire to feed it until my grandmother came to fix breakfast.

My mother developed what these days would be euphemistically called a liquidity problem. Our release from the Žilina concentration camp had been an expensive proposition and her hidden pile of cash had dwindled. My mother shielded me from this knowledge, but I saw how our most modest luxuries were gradually eliminated. To replenish her cash, my enterprising mother went into business, together with her friend Ilush Polak. They procured yarn and started knitting women's hats, which were then in vogue, as well as baby clothes, scarves, and shawls. They soon had the last of the Jewish women working for them, doing piecework in their homes. A friend named Kamila, with a talent for pattern making, became the foreman and teacher. You could bring Kamila any knitted item and she would figure out its stitches and make a pattern, frequently improving upon the original design. The products were marketed through Mrs. Anna Schweidler, a non-Jewish woman who owned a millinery shop. There she sold my mother's and Ilush Polak's products and introduced their line of baby clothes. They actually had to force a 10% commission of the sales upon this incredibly decent woman because she insisted that she did not want to profit from our misfortune. This business was, of course, strictly illegal and could have landed my mother, her workers, and the saintly Mrs. Schweidler in jail.

Once you establish a thriving business, you have to expand it. In order to do so, my mother and Ilush hired a traveling salesman. He was a friend who risked packing a small suitcase with their samples, removing his yellow star (against the law), boarding a train (against the law), traveling to other towns, presenting his wares to various store owners (against the law), and writing orders. When he came back with the orders, my mother's workers filled these, and the salesman made another trip to deliver them, collect the cash and bring it back to the "home office," our living room. Every aspect of these transactions was illegal and entailed tremendous risk but went off without a hitch, as far as I can remember. Business prospered so much that the "firm" started employing non-Jewish women from outlying villages who were happy to make some extra money and were, moreover, in a position to obtain and sell us some scarce food, such as eggs, butter, etc. My mother generally assigned these women the task of producing the large shawls, which was very tedious work, but required the least skill. I, too, was employed, picking up raw material from the wool factory located on the other end of town. Back home I wrapped the raw skeins of wool around two legs of an upturned chair and then wound them into balls. I also delivered finished goods to Mrs. Schweidler's millinery store.

The remaining Jewish families became very close-knit. In spite of the curfew, we visited one another, even in the evenings. To do this, we had to remove our yellow stars and move quickly under cover of darkness. Adko Strassmann came to see us almost daily, bringing news of the progress of the war. This he gathered by visiting some of his non-Jewish friends and listening with them clandestinely to short-wave news broadcasts from Radio London, BBC. We had a map of Europe on which he showed me the frontlines. When I went to bed, he sat with me before I went to sleep and talked to me about whatever was on my mind.

In the fall of 1943 Adko came up with a breathtaking proposal: he would use his contacts to get Paul and me into high school. The Slovaks barred Jewish children from attending their schools and Jewish schools no longer existed. Amazingly enough, Adko succeeded in this plan. The school administration insisted, however, that we first take entrance exams, to see if we, products of the "second-rate" Jewish school, could keep up with the superior Slovak students.

In that school system, all exams were oral.

Snapshot: I am standing in a classroom. On my left is a group of kids sitting at their desks and eyeing me curiously. To my right is a blackboard. I am facing the teacher, who is asking me questions and covering subject after subject. I answer some history questions about the French revolution; I perform some math problems on the blackboard. We cover pretty much every subject. "Music," says the teacher. "Did you take music?" Music consisted simply of learning and singing songs. I answer affirmatively. "OK, sing us a song," says the teacher. My mind goes blank. I know lots of songs, but they all seem to have fled from my memory.

"Well, didn't you sing songs ?"

"Sure we did."

"Well, what kind of songs ?"

"Hebrew songs," I blurt out.

A moment of silence. "Well then, sing us a Hebrew song."

I have a large repertory of Hebrew songs, but my mind is still blank. Then I have an inspiration and launch into the *Hatikvah* (the Jewish national anthem).

The teacher listens to me with an inscrutable expression; the kids listen, open-mouthed. The teacher concludes the exam.

That evening I told Adko the story of my music exam. He did not find it the least bit humorous, but instantly blew up in a rage. This was the only time that I remember him being truly angry with me. He berated me for wasting his enormous expenditure of effort and money to get Paul and me into the school. He was convinced that due to my utter obtuseness all of it was now in vain.

Nevertheless, we were accepted into the school. For a year we studied and even learned, in spite of the totally uncongenial environment.

> **Snapshot:** I am in a science class. The teacher asks the class a question. There is silence. I raise my hand timidly and answer the question correctly.

> "Now, we just discussed this last week," says the teacher irritably. "How is it possible that Kubiček is the only one among you who remembers it ?"

> Silence. Then a boy pipes up, "It's easy for him, he's a Jew."

This is such a perfect illustration of the contradictory mixture of hate and admiration the Slovaks had for Jews. It reminded me of my grandfather's stories of his life as the only Jewish farmer in a small village. While the local peasants typically spent their evenings in bars, drinking the local firewater called *"palene,"* my grandfather stayed home, reading by candlelight, often perusing all the pamphlets about farming that he could obtain. These taught him how to improve the quality and yield of his crop. Thus, for a number of years, he was the first and only farmer in his village to use fertilizer. When his crops did visibly better than those of his neighbors, to the peasants of the village it was proof incontrovertible that it was easy for the Jew since he was allied with the devil.

1944: The Concentration Camps

As 1944 started, we actually began feeling somewhat optimistic. Adko kept listening to Radio London in secret and kept us apprised of the progress and favorable changes in the tides of the war. He explained to us the eagerly awaited concept of the "second front," which the Allies had to initiate in order to defeat the Germans. On June 6th, I remember being at the river with some adult friends, when we spotted Adko running toward us. Breathlessly, he brought us news of the Normandy invasion, the eagerly awaited "second front." This we thought was surely the beginning of the end.

This news also galvanized the Slovak anti-German underground and their groups of armed partisans. Sporadically, these had been active from the start of the war, but in 1944 they gathered strength and became cockier and more active. They moved out of the mountains, attacked the Slovak army and actually liberated one town and established their headquarters there. This insolence the Germans could not tolerate. Considering the Slovak army unreliable, for good reasons, as some army elements actually joined the partisans, the Germans moved their own army into Slovakia and took over the fight against the partisans. They quickly reoccupied the liberated town and soon the partisans were back in the mountains, reduced again to sporadic guerilla warfare.

To their dismay, the German army found that apart from the Jews in forced labor camps, there were still some 20,000 at large in the country. These were people absolutely without property and without any civil rights, but the Germans considered this a serious breach of their vision of a Europe "cleansed" of Jews and they immediately began to rectify this situation. The dread deportations were instituted again, this time organized by the efficient Germans, albeit with the cooperation of the Slovak police and the Hlinka Guard. Alois Brunner, the infamous principal deputy of Adolf Eichmann, was put in charge of the anti-Jewish operation. (For many years, Brunner remained number one on the list of most wanted Nazi war criminals. For a time he was believed to be living in hiding in Syria, though by now is assumed to have died.) He quickly established a concentration camp in the town of Sered. With the Germans now in command, and the Slovaks excluded from decision-making, there were no helpful contacts left to us, as well as nobody to bribe.

Adko Strassmann was the first person arrested in our town, together with his father-in-law, and with the remaining leaders of our community. They were quickly deported and never heard from again. This time, Jews who were not immediately arrested did not wait around, but scattered into hiding places which we called "bunkers." My mother arranged for a bunker in the house of Mrs. Kubinska, a non-Jewish woman who took in four of us: my mother, my grandmother, Adko's wife Franzi, and myself. Mrs. Kubinska was a widow, with a private house situated in a walled-in garden, thus offering what looked like good security, notwithstanding the fact that it was in the center of town. The woman was paid a good deal of money for her effort, but our accommodations were really equivalent to a secret hotel.

The secret did not last long. A few weeks passed quietly. Then one day the doorbell rang and in walked a couple of German soldiers, accompanied by a few Slovak Hlinka Guard members. They advised Mrs. Kubinska that they only wanted to inspect the house, a not unusual occurrence in those days. While she took them to her living quarters, the four of us quickly hid in a small pantry. Then we heard the sound of heavy boots in the kitchen and the pantry door opened. Our time of hiding was over.

We spent the night in the local jail. The following morning Slovak guards escorted the four of us, among about a dozen other Jews, on a passenger train, to the Sered concentration camp.

Our day of deportation came about five days later. We were ordered to line up with our luggage and then forced aboard cattle cars. These were empty, except for a large canister of water on the right side and a large empty can on the left, which was to serve as our toilet. We were packed in tightly. The large doors slid shut with a bang and were bolted from outside. There was one small, barred window on either side of the car, just below the low ceiling. We spent two days and two nights in this cattle car. The conditions are hard to describe. The occupants were families: people of all ages. A mother nursed her infant, while some others were quite elderly. An old woman died during the first night. Her overcoat was pulled across her face and that was that. The train moved very slowly. It spent lengthy periods standing at stations. We ate whatever food we had brought with us. Exhausted from the tension, we slept, as far as this was possible, leaning against one another in seated positions. On a few brief occasions, the guards opened the doors and permitted us to empty our "toilet." This allowed some of the incredible stench to dissipate.

By this time we knew all about the extermination camps, about the gas chambers, about the crematoria and about the fate that awaited us. I do not know just how and when we learned about it, but I well remember that I was fully cognizant of it. A few people kept careful watch of the stations we were passing, trying to determine our train's direction. They soon figured out that we were not heading north towards Poland and its extermination camps, but west, through Austria and into Germany. This news offered us a measure of relief, since we also knew that the

Germans did not run actual extermination camps inside Germany.

In the fall of 1944, the Russian army had fought its way deep into Poland. Seeing the handwriting on the wall, the Germans started liquidating their concentration camps in Poland and transferring the camps' remaining population to camps in Germany proper. Ours was thus one of the first transports routed to Germany rather than to Poland.

We arrived in the camp of Bergen-Belsen. I was in a group of women and children, with my mother and grandmother, exactly the kind of mix which a couple of weeks earlier would have been routed to Auschwitz and gone from the railroad siding directly into the gas chambers. Franzi Strassmann, as a woman alone, had been separated from us already in Camp Sered. We never saw her again. We were now herded into a large barracks, called *Block* in camp parlance, with hundreds of double bunks. An open area in the center contained a small, cast-iron, wood-burning stove. This generated enough heat to enable you to warm your hands if you extended them right above it, but this bit of heat did not augur well for the upcoming winter.

We were immediately introduced to a ubiquitous concentration camp feature: the latrines. There were not many of them. Each was located in a freestanding wooden shed, some distance away from the barracks. Long before you entered it, it would advertise its presence by its unmistakable smell. The shed enclosed a large, rectangular open pit. This was surmounted by a low scaffold, consisting of a horizontal plank about 4" wide on which you would sit; another plank ran along the level of your back; you could lean against it and thus avoid the possibility of toppling backward into the pit of excrement. This construction could accommodate some two dozen people or more at a time. Upon opening the door to the latrine you ran into a putrid wall of intense, sickening stench. This was a place where you did not want to linger beyond absolute necessity.

In spite of the size and depth of the latrine pit, the level of its content kept rising every day. Before it reached the top, it had to be periodically skimmed off and reduced in quantity. A team of prisoners called the *Scheisskommando* — literally, the shit detail — performed this job. They would come pushing a wagon and armed with pails and long-handled tools that looked like giant ladles. They would use these to ladle out the content of the pit into pails and then pour it into the wagon. Then they pushed the wagon to some cesspool I know not where, to be emptied of its odious content. I once listened to the tale of a woman who credited her survival of Auschwitz to having been a member of its *Scheisskommando*. She claimed that they received double food rations. They were also given their own private corner in the barracks since their clothes had gradually absorbed the smell of their job and so everyone gave them a wide berth and left them in peace. Instead of feeling ostracized she looked upon her job with a positive attitude and considered it her passport to survival. Survival from one day to the next was what our existence was all about.

We were allowed to keep our clothes and luggage, an unheard-of luxury in a concentration camp. It was indicated to us that this arrangement was temporary, prior to us being "processed." After two weeks of waiting it seemed to us that we were somehow forgotten. But then it was announced that we were to be divided and integrated into other groups. This time I was classified as an adult and detailed to a group of men. I was barely able to say a quick goodbye to my mother and grandmother, as I hurriedly picked up my possessions and stuffed them into a backpack. For the first time I was separated from my mother, my "Rock of Gibraltar." I was petrified and totally numb. I never felt so desperately alone. It was a feeling that was never to leave me until the moment, after the end of the war, light-years later, when I was reunited with my mother.

Within hours my group of men was loaded into the now-familiar and dreaded cattle car, for a trip that mercifully lasted only about half a day. That evening we arrived in Camp Sachsenhausen, located in a suburb of Berlin called Oranienburg. It was a cool evening and while I bundled up into my warm overcoat, I was surprised to see quite a few prisoners running around dressed in nothing but their pajamas. This was the start of my full integration into the system. I had to part with all my possessions, including the remaining food that we had brought from Slovakia that my mother had pressed upon me. I had to strip off all my clothes. I now joined a long line of naked men, slowly shuffling forward, for what seemed like an hour. Once I finally got to the head of the line I was told to sit down on a wood stool and incline my head forward. A prisoner wielding hand clippers stood behind me. I felt the metal clippers press against the nape of my neck and then glide smoothly across my scalp toward my forehead. A few such passes and my hair lay near my feet. I was then directed to stand up, spread my legs, and stretch my arms to the sides. The hair from my underarms and my pubic hair joined the pile of hair on the ground. (I once read the account of a survivor who had been a barber and was detailed in Auschwitz to clip off the hair of long lines of naked women, work he performed day after day for two years and it thus became his passport to survival.) We were led to showers. This terrified us since by this time we knew that the gas chambers were disguised as showers. According to our information, there were not supposed to be any death chambers in Germany, but still we entered the showers with great trepidation. When actual water started flowing from the showerheads, we felt immensely relieved. After the showers, we were issued clothes and I found out that the "pajamas" that I had seen outdoors were actually striped prison uniforms and would be all I would wear throughout my internment. The boots we received had wooden soles to which canvas uppers were stapled. These forced one to walk in a stiff, ungainly fashion, the standard prisoners' walk. A striped cap completed the outfit. Each of us also received a soup bowl, a cup, and a spoon, all three items made of plain steel, painted black. The bowl had a small hook attached to it, to enable you to clip it to the waistband of your pants. Thus changed in our new attire, I had difficulty recognizing the men I had arrived with. I wondered whether I would recognize my own mother, with her head shaved and clad in a striped shift that women prisoners wore. We were also assigned numbers. Henceforth, my identity was #119,748. So, there you had it: instant dehumanization in three easy steps.

I was housed in a large *Block*, with a few hundred other newly-processed prisoners. We were again reminded that these were only temporary quarters. Another two weeks of limbo followed; nothing much happened. Every day seemed to start shortly after we were allowed to crawl into our bunks — or so it appeared to me: at daybreak the doors to the *Block* burst open noisily, the electric lights came on blindingly, and a small team of prisoners rushed in, brandishing sticks and yelling, *"Alles-auf"* (everybody up) and *"Schnell, schnell"* (quick, quick), as well as *"Shipko, shipko"* (quick, quick, in Polish) and *"Yazda, yazda"* (let's go, move it, in Polish). This was punctuated by loud banging of the sticks against our wooden bunks. Blows could also rain on those who did not immediately spring out of bed. This humble job of waking prisoners was generally given to Poles, even though they were considered to be much inferior to the German prisoners. The job brought with it few benefits and necessitated getting up much earlier than anyone else, so why not give it to the lowly Poles? Actually, Poles made up the second-longest serving group of prisoners, right after the Germans, and this "seniority" enabled them to obtain some of these lowly jobs which became their passports to survival. Polish also became the second-most important language in the camps. My knowledge of Slovak and Czech enabled me to make out some of the Polish — all of these are Slavic languages — and I quickly picked up some essential

Polish vocabulary, including a repertoire of truly vulgar swear-words, a useful knowledge at times.

The third most important language was Russian since Russians formed another sizable minority in the camps. A lot of them were former prisoners of war who were transferred to concentration camps as punishment for insubordination. Russians formed a very cohesive group, loyal to their officers who continued to command them even in the camps. The Germans found them difficult to control, except with utmost brutality. In a later camp, which had a large Russian population, I was befriended by a couple of them and they enabled me to pick up some Russian, too, and add to my international vocabulary of pungent curses. In return, I found that they were eager for my help in teaching them German. A memorable sentence uttered by my friend Grishka, in his inimitable, idiosyncratic German, will forever stick in my mind, "I ten more years in camp sitting — everything German speaking."

One morning, after we had lined up for our usual morning *Appell*, or roll call, we were ordered to remain standing. We stood and stood. Rumor had it that we were going to be transferred either to another section, or to another camp.

In my memory of the concentration camps, I clearly recall each individual camp and its conditions. Particular moments and incidents remain etched in my mind and stand out like the snapshots I wrote about earlier. I can see every detail in my mind's eye; I can feel, I can smell the moment. I can describe it minutely. There are, however, certain scenes of brutality and horror that I am simply unable to verbalize. I cannot block them from my memory, but there they will have to remain buried.

Of the snapshots I can recount, here is one scene in Sachsenhausen:

Hundreds of us stand in long, five-deep rows. Our ranks are strictly enforced, but we are allowed to stand at ease. I am in a front row. It is quite cold and I am getting colder and colder as time passes. We all keep moving from foot to foot, hands in the pockets. Every once in a while I take my hands out of my pockets and clap my arms vigorously around my shoulders in order to warm up my entire body, until my bare fingers get numb from the cold. I shove my hands back into my pockets and move my fingers, until I can feel them again and then go back to slapping my shoulders. When my nose runs, I wipe the length of my sleeve across it.

In front of us stand a few German *Prominenter* prisoners. These are men of privilege who are high above us in the camp hierarchy. Many of them are criminals who have been transferred from jail to the camps. They have absolute power over us ordinary prisoners. Their power has bred in them an arrogance and, frequently, a brutality matching that of their Nazi masters. One of them comes over to me and asks me whether I speak German. I was completely bilingual as a child, as fluent in German as in Slovak. This language facility was of incalculable advantage to me in the concentration camp. So this *Prominenter* prisoner begins chatting with me, while I keep shifting from foot to foot. Owing to his rank, he wears good, warm clothes, gloves, a warm hat, leather shoes. He sees in front of him a miserably cold little boy. Though fourteen years old, I am small for my age, I look younger, and I guess one could say that I am a fairly cute kid. By this point of the war, the majority of cute Jewish kids have long since breathed their last inhaling Zyklon-B poison gas, so I am also a rarity. Suddenly, this German prisoner peels off his wool gloves and hands them to me. It takes me a while to comprehend that he means me to have them. I stand astonished and ready to cry over this overwhelming act of generosity. About ten minutes later, we are given the order to start marching. I have just enough time to wave a gloved hand to my benefactor.

After a march of several hours, we arrived at a new camp, Heinkel. Here we waited for several more hours in the cold, before going through the ritual of being processed as new camp arrivals. Again we lost all our clothes, such as they were at this point, and entered showers with unease and fear. Once we were issued new clothes, I was no longer the proud possessor of a pair of gloves, a scant half-day after I acquired this luxury.

Our accommodations at this camp were the worst I experienced. Heinkel was the large bomber aircraft factory with a slave labor camp attached. By this period of the war, the factories had been bombed into oblivion by the Allied air forces and aircraft production had ceased, but some giant aircraft hangars remained. We were housed in one of these hangars that had concrete floors, very high steel walls and a steel roof. We slept in a section of the hangar that had some loose straw on the floor. The hundreds of prisoners generated no warmth in this huge, frigid space. My sleeping method was as follows: Each prisoner had been issued one blanket. I teamed up with a boy my age whose name was Artur. We folded one blanket in half and put it on the bit of straw as our mattress, to insulate us from the cold floor. On this we lay down, close together, and wrapped ourselves tightly in our other blanket. To generate some warmth, one of us put his head under the blanket and commenced breathing heavily. Once he started to suffocate he surfaced and the other one went under to repeat the process. This way we managed to warm our little "tent." Then we slept with the blanket drawn at least partially over our heads.

There were three feelings that were ever-present in a concentration camp. The first one was hunger. You just never felt really sated. Hunger gnawed your insides and seemed to consume you from within. You licked your bowl over and over after each meal of turnip soup. You kept sucking your spoon for any possible remnant of flavor. Thoughts of food were always on your mind. In prisons, talk in the evenings reputedly revolves around sex; in the concentration camps, talk turned mainly around food. Sex was not an issue. Malnutrition effectively kills the libido. Women, incidentally, soon lost their menstrual cycles, a fact which, I imagine, they must have regarded as a blessing in disguise. A quiet evening would begin with someone saying, "You know what I like?" This would be followed by a loving description of some food or dish. Others would chime in, contributing their food dreams. It generally ended by someone yelling, "Shut up, already! Stop torturing us with this constant talk of food." Then all would be quiet again.

The second was a feeling of weariness, of continuous physical exhaustion. Given the opportunity of sitting on a bench at a table, you would rest your arms upon the table, then your head on your arms and the next thing you knew you were asleep. Whereupon, the next thing you felt was a sharp poke in the ribs and you heard a loud command to stay awake. Sleep was only allowed when we were ordered to do so. I did manual labor at this camp for only three long days. I was part of a group that was building underground bomb shelters. I still have a mental snapshot of five of us carrying a long, heavy log on our shoulders: that is, the four men shouldered the log, while I, being small, had to stretch out my arms above my head merely to make contact with the log. I thus contributed very little to carrying its weight. We dropped the log next to the work site and, as it hit the frozen ground with a thud, one of the men, a young strapping guy, spat out, "A couple of months ago I could have carried this all by myself like nothing and just look at me now!"

Due to our debilitation, the work we performed was really most inefficient. Even though the hundreds of slave labor camps that dotted the landscape of Germany were created ostensibly to provide cheap labor for their industrial enterprises, and the large wrought iron gates at the entrance of major camps carried the slogan *Arbeit Macht Frei* — "Work Makes You Free" — the ultimate purpose of a slave labor camp was not labor but slavery. The industrial firms that participated and acquiesced in this system were a veritable who's who of German industry. Among them were some companies well-known today outside of Germany, such as BMW, Volkswagen, Shell, Siemens.... Their management understood perfectly well that we were totally expendable; that as soon as they lost any of these workers there were always plenty more where they came from. None of these firms had any objection to the use of slave labor: it was, after all, free and thus contributed to their bottom line. Nor, to my knowledge, was there any instance of any of these civilian enterprises making the least attempt to alleviate the lot of its slave laborers.

The third feeling that continually enveloped you was that of terror. There was always something terrifying going down nearby: you heard shouted commands, swearing in German and in a gamut of languages, cries of pain, begging for mercy. You just cowered and hoped that whatever was happening would not involve you. You tended to withdraw into yourself and isolate yourself from others. I became like a little animal, quailing in its burrow, wary and distrustful of everyone and yet I had to extend my trust to those who were willing to help me.

There was a danger in withdrawing too deeply into oneself. There were those who withdrew to the point of becoming totally indifferent to their surroundings and uncommunicative.

They entered a lethargic state, readily identifiable. There was a name for such a person and it was *Muselmann*. This translates as Muslim; in fact, the English word "mussulman" is the archaic version of Muslim, but its use in this case had nothing whatever to do with the Moslem religion. The origin of the German use of the word is obscure. It appears to have originated in Auschwitz where there actually was a barracks called *Muselmannblock*. Prisoners consigned to it were recognized as useless for any further work and had only one destination: the gas chamber. The expression became common to all camps. When you saw someone who had entered this state of physical and mental decrepitude, you recognized him instantly as a *Muselmann* and you knew that as such he was doomed to die soon.

In such a state, death may have seemed as a release from constant suffering. Faced with a continuous, unrelieved life of pain and terror, one could think that death could be looked upon as an acceptable — welcome even — way to end it all. Yet suicide in the concentration camp, though possible, was rare. There was even an expression for easy suicide, "walking into the wire." Each camp was surrounded by a high barbed wire fence through which coursed high voltage electricity. Touch the fence and you are out of your misery. So, why would you not take this way out? Here is the answer: the instinct for self-preservation. This is a most powerful instinct residing deep within each of us, common to us, as well as to all animals. The vast majority of people will never come face to face with it in their lifetime. It only surfaces in extreme circumstances. That is why some people sometimes manage to survive against staggering odds and that is why we persevered and went on with our miserable, worthless lives from day to day. It explains how people survived calamities throughout history and how people survive catastrophes and cruelties today, whether caused by man or by nature.

Snapshot: Groups of prisoners have been ordered to one section of the hangar. Names, rather than numbers, are called out, for assignment to *Kommandos* (work details). The named prisoners step forward and are assigned to a particular detail. My name is called. I step forward. From inside one of the groups I hear a small boy's voice calling out, "Peter Kubiček?" A boy pushes his way to the front of the group and I recognize my friend from Trenčín, Franzo Goldner.

I met Franzo when we were six years old at the start of elementary school. We immediately took to each other and became totally inseparable for the ensuing years. In 1942 his was one of the first families to be deported to the Žilina camp. His father managed to get a job on the camp's repair crew. Through this job he was able to exempt his family from the weekly deportations to the Auschwitz gas chambers. When the deportations ended, they were interned in the Novaky forced-labor camp. There they spent close to two years, until the camp was liberated by the Slovak partisans. The able-bodied young Jewish men joined the partisans, including Franzo's older brother. The families, however, had nowhere to go and fled into hiding in the mountains. Before long, however, the Germans rounded them up and deported them to German camps.

So, after a separation of some 2½ years, my best friend Franzo and I meet in the Heinkel concentration camp. By this time I no longer slept on the concrete floor. A kind *Prominenter* had obtained for me an actual bunk in a small partitioned-off room. I now begged him to get a bed for my friend Franzo, too. As no spare bunk was available, my protector told me that Franzo could sleep with me as long as we were willing to share my narrow bunk. For the next few nights the men in the room had to keep hushing the two of us as we could not stop talking and recounting our experiences of the preceding years.

My stay at Camp Heinkel lasted for two months or so. Once again a group of us was transferred, this time to Camp

Inak, located in Siemensstadt, home of the giant Siemens factories. (Today this company is considerably more giant, a multinational industrial powerhouse, notwithstanding its history as a major supporter of Hitler's war effort and of having been intimately affiliated with a number of slave labor camps.)

* * *

The bulk of the preceding account was written in November, 2000. I now continue with the memoir written originally for my daughters in 1983.

PETER KUBICEK

For Mia and Katia

A birthday makes you feel special. You feel different from other people when your family and friends celebrate you on this, your very own special day. And yet, as your birthdays pass, you may find it difficult to remember just how you spent that day a few years hence. Do you remember exactly how you spent, say, your 11th or 12th birthday? What will you remember of your 15th in a few years?

For some very special reasons, I remember my 15th birthday with a clarity that the intervening 38 years cannot dim. I thought I would set down my remembrances of that time, so you can share them and have this permanent record of them.

I spent the day of January 26, 1945, lying on a cot in the *Revier* (sick bay) of the German concentration camp Haselhorst, which was located in the town of Siemensstadt, a suburb of Berlin. At this point, the Second World War had gone on for an incredibly long five-and-a-half years. Now, however, we knew that the end must be near; that the defeat of Germany was just a matter of time; and that if we could just survive a few more months our nightmare would finally be over. That knowledge gave me a strength that my body otherwise lacked.

I had been advertising my impending birthday for some time to friends at the camp. I could not quite believe the reality of what was happening to me: that I was about to spend my birthday in this surreal place, far from my mother, my father, my other family and friends with whom I had grown up. I did not know where any of them were or even whether they were still alive.

My friends in the camp were of two groups. Four of the ten boys of my age with whom I shared a room were from Slovakia. Our room was small and had just enough space for four three-tiered bunks arranged in a U-shape around a central table with two benches and a narrow closet with cubbyholes for our meager possessions. But this was a luxurious suite compared to how the other prisoners were housed. All prisoners in camps generally lived in barracks. The barracks were long, single-story wooden buildings. The inside held one, or sometimes two, large rectangular rooms, crowded with long rows of bunks in three tiers. Sometimes there was space for a few long tables and benches and that was it. There were no closets or lockers of any kind and ordinarily prisoners had to keep whatever little they owned on their persons at all times, if they did not want their things stolen. In this way hundreds of prisoners lived and slept together in one room. In charge of each *Block* (barracks), was a *Blockälteste* (literally, block elder). Although himself a prisoner, he had a very powerful job. He was in charge of all the other prisoners of his block when they were not working; he had complete power over them. He lived in a separate room that served as both his office and his home. My particular block in Haselhorst had an additional room in front of the office of the *Blockälteste* and that was where we so-called *Jugendliche* (juveniles) lived.

My second category of friends at Haselhorst were a few adult *Prominente*. These were very useful people to know. They were privileged prisoners who held the good jobs in a camp. The *Blockälteste* was one of the most prominent. Others included the *Vorarbeiter*, or foreman, who was in charge of a *Kommando*, a prisoner work party; those who worked in the kitchen, or the clothing warehouse, the sick bay, or the central camp office. There was a hierarchy of different grades of *Prominente* in each camp. Most of these were German, non-Jewish prisoners. The *Prominente* had easier work, more and better food, better clothes and thus a much better chance of survival. The next best thing was to become friendly with a *Prominenter* and get a low-ranking special job from him, such as helping with food distribution, running errands and the like.

Prior to Haselhorst I had been in a nearby camp called Inak, also located in Siemensstadt. There I had become a *Kalfaktor*, or helper, of a *Blockälteste* named Willi Nehring. This man no doubt saved my life when he picked me out of the horde of prisoners to be his helper. Willi was a German; this was his twelfth year in the concentration camp. As distinct from the majority of prisoners who were considered "political," Willi had been an ordinary criminal. Soon after the Nazis came to power in Germany, they created concentration camps for Jews, as well as for people they considered enemies, or politically unreliable. They soon came to the conclusion that it was a waste to run prisons for ordinary criminal prisoners, in addition to concentration camps for political prisoners and so, for the sake of efficiency, Germany simply transferred its entire prison population to the concentration camps.

The plain criminals became the "elite" of the camps, with the pick of the best jobs. They were classified into two groups: the *Leichtverbrecher* (petty criminals) and *Schwerverbrecher* (serious or dangerous offenders). Every prisoner had sewn onto his jacket his inmate number and a sign designating the type of prisoner he was. My sign was a red triangle pointing downward, to show I was a political prisoner; and above it a yellow horizontal stripe, to show I was a Jew. Next to these symbols was my name: 119748. The *Leichtverbrecher* wore green triangles pointing down;

the *Schwerverbrecher* green triangles pointing up. Willi was one of the first criminals transferred to the camps from the prisons; his green triangle pointed resolutely upward. When I asked him what he did before prison, he just smiled and said he had been a *Spitzbub* (a rascal). He was unusually good with his hands and could fix anything. I could picture him as a locksmith or a safecracker; he would have made a very good burglar. To my mind, he was also the most decent, most honest and kind human being I met in the eight different camps of which I was an inmate.

As *Blockaelteste*, Willi had his own room which served as his office and bedroom. In the given circumstances, the room had some positively luxurious touches of civilization. It had its own small sink with running cold water, with a mirror above it. He had soap, a comb (he was permitted to grow hair!), a toothbrush, a razor. It was here that I had the experience of seeing myself in a mirror for the first time in months. I was shocked by the unfamiliar image that stared back at me. Apart from my bare, shaven skull and my shrunken, emaciated face, it was my eyes that I hardly recognized. They were deeply sunken in my skull and had a haunted expression that looked totally alien to me. I avoided the mirror thereafter.

One of Willi's unvarying daily chores was the distribution of bread rations — literally our staple of life, always anticipated with an eagerness bordering on desperation. Every afternoon a bin containing some 50–60 loaves of bread was delivered into his direct care. Each loaf weighed one kilogram, which is about 2.2 pounds. It was Willi's important duty to divide each of these loaves into five portions. He started off by carefully sharpening his large knife. He then had one assistant at the right end of the table slide over one loaf at a time. With great speed and machine-like precision, Willi's knife bit into the loaf four times, resulting in five portions of about equal weight. Another assistant at the left end of the table scooped up the portions into another waiting bin. So it continued until all loaves were divided. But every so often, Willi made an extra cut of one single slice which was destined for a separate container. These slices were his private hoard and wealth. It was ample to serve as food for him and enabled him to distribute some of it at will to his helpers — that included me, of course — and to his friends, or to whomever he wanted to remunerate. Bread was the hallowed currency of the concentration camp. It made you rich and influential and powerful.

As in Haselhorst, at Inak the *Jugendliche* were housed in a separate room of one of the blocks. When Willi picked me as his *Kalfaktor*, he arranged my transfer to his block, where there was another room housing a group of somewhat older *Jugendliche*. These were some twenty 18- to 20-year-olds and their room was right opposite Willi's. There I got one of the preferred lower bunks. A rather strange character, called "Zigeuner Franz" (Frank, the Gypsy) also shared this room. He was a German gypsy, in his mid-twenties, a sort of semi-*Prominenter*. Although he had a better job, the other Germans who considered gypsies the lowest rank of humanity, barely above Jews, ostracized him. For this reason he was not housed with other German prisoners, but with my group of Jewish boys. He considered that placement to be an insult and way below his station. He studiously avoided all contact with us Jewish boys and only came in to sleep in his small separate area near the entrance of our room, where he had his own freestanding bed, without any bunks either above nor right next to it.

Zigeuner Franz had an article of clothing which in our circumstances was quite rare: an overcoat. It was beige, in a herringbone pattern, and several sizes too large for him. This did not bother him. He cinched its belt tightly around his waist, while its hem trailed close to the ground. He cut a comical figure wearing it, though it undoubtedly must have kept him warm. Every night he went through a ritual of folding it carefully and laying it across the foot of his bunk, where he could guard it. On cold nights, he spread it across his blanket.

The German SS Guards called him *Zigeuner Franz, der Judenschreck* (Frank the Gypsy, Scourge of the Jews). His specialty was group or mass torture. What is group torture? you may ask. If, say, you want to inflict physical punishment on a group of 100-200 people, beating them individually would be prohibitively laborious and tiring. Even the most industrious SS guards might be hard pressed to keep up a sufficient level of enthusiasm if they had to torture 100-200 people consecutively. So, the SS devised a better method. They would take out the group designated for punishment to the *Appellplatz* (inspection square), where they would arrange them in a circle, with Zigeuner Franz in the center. He would then yell out commands to the circle of prisoners, instructing them to perform various physical exercises. SS Guards would surround the group, armed with clubs, and "encourage" the laggards. The SS officers, who invariably found the scene hugely entertaining, stood around and watched. Other prisoners were forced to stand in ranks along the sides and watch the proceedings as an object lesson of what could be in store for them.

Zigeuner Franz had a most fertile imagination when it came to devising exercises that were excruciatingly difficult and tiring for the weakened, emaciated prisoners. The guards used their clubs to mercilessly beat those who could not keep up with Franz's commands. This performance went on until the SS officers were satisfied with the number of beaten, lifeless bodies they saw on the ground, or until they grew tired of the amusement. Afterwards they congratulated Zigeuner Franz on a job well done, particularly if he had come up with new "tricks." Franz beamed in their approbation.

> **Snapshot:** It is late afternoon and I am lying on my bunk, shivering with cold. I have a high fever and feel alternately very hot and then very cold. I am now

shivering so much that my teeth chatter and my bunk rattles. Zigeuner Franz walks in. He takes in the scene.

"What's with you?" he asks.

"I d-don't know, I just feel v-very v-very c-cold," I manage to say.

Franz says nothing more. He takes off his prized overcoat. Suddenly, he unfurls it above my bunk and spreads it over my blanket, still without saying a word. Amazed, I thank him through my chattering teeth.

I also have a particular memory one SS lieutenant. He was a big, blond brute of a guy, epitome of the Nazi master race. He always paraded around in long strides, with a scowl on his face, looking to find an infraction, real or imagined, which would give him an excuse to beat up or kick around some hapless prisoner who caught his malevolent eye. Whenever he came around, you just whipped off your cap, stood at attention and hoped he would pass by without looking at you. In my memory (with apology to William Styron) I have dubbed him *Scharfuehrer Schweinehund*. This translates roughly as Lieutenant Filthy Swine, but in German it is a more common and evocative expression. He remains for me the image of a quintessential sadist.

Snapshot: I am part of a small detail of prisoners, walking from Inak to Haselhorst, where we have been sent to fetch something. There are about eight or ten of us, guarded by two SS guards with rifles, and led by *Scharfuehrer Schweinehund*. We are walking on a dusty road that runs along the outskirts of the town. On our left is open countryside; on our right are backyard gardens of a long row of one-family houses, fenced in by chain-link. Nobody else is on the road, except up ahead a small boy of about three or four years who is playing in the dust. A large dog, inside one of the backyards ahead of us, suddenly bounds toward the fence, jumping up and barking furiously. The little boy gets frightened and starts crying. *Schweinehund* reacts by running toward him. He kneels in the dust next to the boy, strokes his head and talks to him gently. The little boy stops crying. When our group passes them, the lieutenant straightens up and comes along with us. He keeps turning back, though, waving to the boy, smiling benevolently.

I mulled over this image for a long time. The fact that this sadist had a human side caught me totally by surprise. I now imagined him going home to visit his family, his children crawling all over him, overjoyed at seeing their loving daddy. I realized that this man operated on two distinct levels, akin to two faucets, one marked "human" and one "inhuman" and he could turn them on and off at will. His inhumanity now seemed much worse to me than when I had taken him for a sadist, pure and simple.

We were in camp Inak that Christmas. I recall it vividly for several reasons. First of all, the SS actually decided to treat us to a better dinner than usual: it consisted of boiled cabbage and boiled potatoes. More importantly, the portions were larger than usual.

A *Blockaelteste* like Willi would be visited daily by one or another SS *Scharführer* who acted as his supervisor. Willi had a surprisingly cordial relationship with one of them, a somewhat older man, named Siebenhaar. Theirs was a finely calibrated master/slave connection which Willi shrewdly exploited. A few days before Christmas, Willi had asked Siebenhaar for permission to arrange a Christmas party for his *Block*. He also told him of a Hungarian gypsy prisoner who had reputedly been a master fiddler prior to his incarceration, and innocently asked if he would be able to procure a loan of a violin for the Christmas party. To my great astonishment *Scharführer* Siebenhaar not only approved Willi's plan, but arrived the next day carrying a violin.

That evening Willi called in the gypsy, whose name was Janos (pronounced Yanosh). When Janos saw the violin his eyes widened; he grabbed the instrument and immediately started playing it, a beatific smile spreading across his face. I never saw a prisoner in a concentration camp as deliriously happy as this man was at that moment.

For the party, Willi chose the center of the *Block* where the tables for our meals were located. He invited some of his green-triangle friends, as well as the small group of *Jugendliche* from the next *Block*. Other prisoners were encouraged to contribute some skill to the party, but nobody was capable of summoning up the energy for the talent show, except one man who composed and performed a song for the occasion. The form and melody of the song was familiar to me from my early childhood experiences in the *Hashomer Hatzair*. The object was to compose two-line rhyming couplets spoofing our leaders. The aim was to be brief and witty. After each couplet the entire audience would sing an essentially nonsensical refrain. In the song this man wrote he made gentle fun of the green-triangle *Prominente*.

I clearly recall the couplet he sang about Willi. It went like this:

"Der Blockleiter Willi gestand es mir offen,
Ich hab' meine Stimme schön längst versoffen."

Free translation in rhyme:
"Blockleader Willi admitted by choice,
Many years ago booze ruined my voice."

Then the assembled prisoners would chime in with the refrain. OK, you'd have to have been there, in the surreal circumstances, to find this particularly witty. What's remarkable to me is that a prisoner would find the inner strength to meet the challenge of composing verses. In any case, it made such an impression on me that 68 years later I can still dredge up this ditty from my memory and can sing it.

Then Janos started playing and singing Hungarian songs. He was capable of playing the violin and singing simultaneously, a talent he perfected before the War when he performed in the cabarets of Budapest. I have never since come across anyone else who could do this.

At one point the gypsy started playing a Hungarian song called "*Fekete Peter*" — Black Peter. Suddenly, my friend Artur, who was sitting next to me on the edge of an upper bunk, jumped down onto a table and launched into a flawless Hungarian rendition of this song, in a confident tenor voice. Deafening applause ensued.

Scharführer Siebenhaar came back the next morning to pick up the violin. Willi expressed his deep gratitude to the SS-man for making this party possible. He added that in the twelve years of his imprisonment this had been the best Christmas he has ever had.

Camp Inak was disbanded when Allied bombing had taken its toll on all German factories, including Siemens, for whose benefit this camp was run. After the destruction of their factories, they needed less slave labor. All Inak prisoners were transferred to different camps. Willi managed to pull some strings to have me included among those who were transferred to nearby Haselhorst, the larger of the two Siemens concentration camps. He knew this camp well and had contacts there among his fellow "green triangles." However, because here he was demoted to an assistant *Blockälteste,* he was not in a position to give me a job. Even so, he did manage to introduce me to his friends and to keep an eye on me. His block was not far from where my group of *Jugendliche* was quartered and I frequently managed to sneak out for a visit to Willy. There I had a chance to sit quietly in the non-threatening atmosphere of his room, next to a warm stove, munch on treats he always had for me, and listen to his pep-talks with which he tried to dispel my oft-present blues.

A few days before my birthday I had become ill during the daily *Appell* (roll-call). Every camp had a large open space called the *Appellplatz*, where all prisoners lined up each morning, *Block* by *Block*, in rows of five, to be counted by the SS officers. The final count had to tally with the official number of prisoners. When the count did not match, which was frequent, there were interminable recounts. This sometimes necessitated searching every single block for a prisoner who may have been hiding, or too sick and weak to get off his bunk, or dead. The SS did not care whether you were alive or dead; they just had this mania for accuracy and the head count had to be dead right. While all this counting and recounting went on, we had to keep standing in exact, neat rows, no matter what the weather. This was January: the weather was customarily cold. If you could have taken a look at such an *Appell*, you would have seen thousands of standing prisoners, dressed in their striped blue-gray uniforms, in their striped caps, stomping their feet in their wood-soled shoes, moving their arms, trying to keep warm.

After standing for what seemed like an eternity, I all of a sudden passed out. When I came to I was lying on the ground. A couple of my friends picked me up immediately and supported me under my arms until the *Appell* was over. Afterward they got permission from our *Blockälteste* to take me to the *Revier* (sick bay). The *Revier* was the camp hospital, but as a hospital it was a joke. It consisted of an examining room, and a larger room with cots or bunks for the sick. Several prisoners who were doctors worked here and even wore white coats. They had among them one stethoscope, a pair of scissors, a knife, some bandages, tongue depressors, a bottle of iodine, and a bottle of aspirin. I do not think I have left out much out of the inventory of medical supplies. The doctor who examined me happened to come from Slovakia and he asked me more questions about where I came from and whom I knew than about how and what I felt. Everyone was in poor physical condition and he could see that I was feverish. He put me to bed and out of kindness managed to keep me there for a week, during which time I had a good rest and regained a little strength. The best thing about being in the *Revier* was that it exempted me from taking part in the daily *Appell*.

The *Revier* was essentially a warehouse for very sick prisoners. Here you either got better, more or less by yourself, and then were able to walk out; or you died in relative peace and were carried out feet first. The bunks were single since the sick prisoners would not have been able to climb to an upper bunk. Each morning I noticed a prisoner walking along the serried bunks, followed by two helpers, giving each of us a cold stare and then walking on. I had no idea who they were or what their function was, until a fellow patient explained to me that they were the *Leichenkommando* — the corpse detail. They were here to pull dead prisoners from their bunks and carry them out onto a waiting wagon. Their problem was that it was often difficult to tell sick, immobile prisoners from dead ones. But this foreman had a system: he carried a stick with a nail sticking out of its end. When he came to a bunk whose occupant gave no sign of life, he lifted the sick man's blanket to uncover his bare feet and then poked a sole of his foot with the sharp point of his stick. If the foot twitched, he walked on. If it didn't, he jabbed again, harder. Absent further reaction, he motioned to his helpers to pull the corpse out.

That is where I spent my fifteenth birthday. The highpoint of the day was a visit from Willi and two of his friends. Willi had found out where I was and did not forget my special day. He and his friends brought me some treats to eat. I have no recollection of the food, but I do remember how excited I was that I should actually receive good wishes and presents under these grim circumstances. In the afternoon my buddies, Artur and Miki, sneaked in and I was equally pleased to see them.

Another visit, from Jusek, was one that really surprised me. Jusek was a Polish boy, two years older than I. He was the only non-Jew in our room of *Jugendliche*. He enjoyed certain privileges just by virtue of being a Gentile and that gave him a clear sense of superiority to us Jewish boys. He had been condemned to the concentration camp for the crime of *Schleichhandel* (black marketeering). This put him into a small category of prisoners called *Asoziale* (antisocial ones). They wore a black identifying triangle next to their number. Jusek was also my boss.

Jusek's main job was to clean the rooms of the SS officers. A special pass allowed him to exit through the main camp gate every morning, pass the rolls of barbed wire and the electrified fence, and go to the adjoining officers' quarters. He swept their rooms, made their beds, and washed their laundry. His other important job was to darn the officers' socks. I do not know how many pairs of wool socks the German army allowed its officers, but it was obvious from the large quantity of socks with holes that Jusek brought back to our room for mending, that the war had lasted longer than Hitler had expected. Jusek brought a load of socks with him every afternoon and went to work darning them. Some of these socks had the most enormous holes. Some had the complete heel or toe end missing. For such large holes Jusek had a special darning technique: he would insert a cup into the sock and then darn around the hole in a circular fashion and so eventually reweave the missing heel or toe. I was fascinated by his work and kept watching how he did it. He soon asked me to help him and I jumped at the chance. Thus I became Jusek's assistant sock darner. He always had plenty of customers and with my help, Jusek was able to more than double his output.

Jusek was paid in food and he shared some of it with me. Compared with our prison diet, the German officers' food was *haute cuisine*. Our standard food ration consisted of the following: in the morning we got our tin cup filled with "coffee." What this black, bitter liquid was made of I do not know; we were simply grateful for the fact that it was hot. For lunch we formed long lines with our metal bowls and snaked our way toward a huge cauldron containing turnip soup. In the evening, the identical repast was called dinner. Occasionally, some dead horses were delivered to the camp kitchen and their meat was chopped up and added to the boiling vats of turnip soup. To find a few small pieces of horsemeat in your soup made for a lucky day. In the evening we also received our daily portion of bread, the equivalent of about four slices. There were two schools of thought about how to consume your bread portion. One was to devour it all for dinner in the hope of coming close to filling your stomach once a day. The other was to hoard it, eat a small piece at a time, and make it last until the next evening. I adhered to the latter school and always kept some of my bread for breakfast and for lunch. Occasionally, in place of turnip soup we had cabbage soup. As a rare treat we got boiled potatoes. These were old rejects; some had frozen before they were relegated to prison food, and they were boiled in their wrinkled, elephantine skin. When we received these precious potatoes, the main question was whether or not to eat them skin and all. I found their slimy skin so disgusting that I gagged on it. But my discards always found customers.

My sock-mending job lasted for the duration of my stay in Haselhorst. Aside from this, as I worked right next to the office of the *Blockälteste*, I was also on call for him as a messenger. This job was most useful since it enabled me to get around the whole camp and to get to know it well, and also to get to know the right people. It also meant tips. A fine tip for an errand was a slice of bread.

Snapshot: I am in the office of a *Blockälteste* to whom I have just delivered something. He is sitting at a table that serves as his desk. He has barely acknowledged me, but says to one of his assistants, "Give him a slice."

The assistant is a kid who hands me not a slice, but a ration of bread.

"I said a slice, not a ration," growls the *Blockälteste*. I freeze. I stand with my right hand outstretched, holding the bread ration between thumb and forefinger. The *Blockälteste* throws me glance. *"Ach, soll er jubeln "* ("Eh, let him exult"), he says and dismisses me with a regal wave of his hand. Elated, I run out as fast as I can, clutching my princely tip.

Food was worth more than any valuable. I was able to barter my extra food and gradually obtain a second blanket, better clothes and even the utter luxury of a pair of leather shoes. Through my sock business I also became acquainted with a number of SS officers who got into the habit of dropping off their work directly with me. This annoyed Jusek tremendously because he wanted to be in charge and keep control of our business.

This existence came to a dramatic end one day in early April when American bombs dropped on the camp instead of on the Siemens factories. The camp was close to the factories where most of the prisoners worked as slave laborers. Allied air raids had been frequent. Almost every night we were woken by air raid sirens. The instant the sirens started wailing, our lights went on for exactly one minute, during which time we had to throw on our clothes and make our way on the run into the air raid shelter. This had become such a routine that sliding off my bunk and getting into my outer clothes became almost a reflex action. We generally continued dozing while sitting in the shelters, unless the noise of exploding bombs kept us awake. Practically every night there were British planes overhead and during the days the planes were American. (Not that we could tell them apart. This was information I learned later.) This time the bombs hit the camp. When we emerged from the bomb shelter, we saw that many barracks were in flames. Instead of reconstructing the camp, the Germans decided to abandon it and moved us to Camp Sachsenhausen.

This camp was closer to Berlin. It was a huge camp, the first concentration camp expressly designed and built for its purpose. In preparation for the 1936 Berlin Olympics, Hitler decreed to build the largest and most imposing Olympic stadium the world had ever seen. It was built in 1935 in Charlottenburg, a suburb to the west of Berlin. In 1936, while the Olympic games were in progress, not far away, in the northern Berlin suburb of Oranienburg, the concentration camp of Sachsenhausen was being constructed by its own inmates. It was to serve as a model for all concentration camps. It was built in the shape of an equilateral triangle, with the *Appellplatz* in its center, and the *Blocks* ranged around it.

While at the Olympics races were run on the state-of-the-art track, while athletic records were broken, and German athletes accepted their medals with their right arms outstretched in the *Heil Hitler* salute, at Sachsenhausen an ingenious track was also constructed. It featured a variety of surfaces and its dual purpose was to test military footwear and to inflict mass torture. Prisoners condemned to the so-called *Schuhprüf Kommando* — the shoe testing detail — walked daily around the track, carrying heavy backpacks, to test how long each type of footwear would last under various controlled conditions and how long the prisoners would last before dying of exhaustion. Meticulous daily records were kept of the type of footwear tested, the weight of the backpacks, the distance covered.

The latter part of the War became a time of tremendous shortages in Germany, as the country was naturally cut off from imports from outside of its sphere of dominance. The new word *Ersatz*, or substitute, came into use. The Germans were desperately trying to invent *ersatz* materials, such as synthetic leather for shoes, rubber for tires, even foods. *Ersatz* coffee, for instance, became the norm. Shoes made of *ersatz* leather would be tested here. *Ersatz* prisoners were, of course, always readily available.

The headquarters of the entire concentration camp system was moved here from the center of Berlin, along with the Gestapo interrogation and torture chambers. It was intended as a standard for other camps. It became a training center for the SS who would afterwards be often sent to oversee other camps. It was called the *Mutterlager*, or mother camp, of its more than 100 sub-camps which surrounded Berlin. At this time it contained about 35,000 prisoners. I was not fully aware in what way this camp served as a "model," unless it was in the many ways you could be punished for any real or imaginary infraction. You could get a severe impromptu beating at any time; you could get a more formal flogging in the center of the *Appellplatz*, with the other prisoners ranged around at attention to witness your pain; you could be shot, gassed, or hanged — these were more or less daily occurrences. In a corner section of the *Appellplatz* was an area that looked to me like a soccer field, with regulation goal posts. I never saw any soccer game being played here, but I witnessed the crossbeams of the soccer goals used as a gallows for public hangings. After the execution, the unfortunates were left twisting there, their feet barely off the ground, each man with a sign around his neck advertising the infraction for which he paid the price; and we would be forced to march past them, to absorb the lesson being taught that day. So I guess the camp was indeed a model of what the Nazis considered to be order, efficiency, and practicality.

For the transfer we went through the usual camp procedure: strip, get your head and body hair shaved, enter showers. Once again I lost all the possessions I had acquired so meticulously and with so much risk. In Haselhorst I actually obtained "civilian" clothes. By the latter part of the war, the Germans apparently stopped bothering to produce new prisoner uniforms and instead recycled some old clothes taken from newly arrived prisoners. But in order that an escaped prisoner could not blend in with the population if he wore civilian clothes, these had to be first adapted for their new purpose. My jacket had a large Jewish yellow star painted on its back with thick smears of enamel paint. My pants had about a one-inch wide stripe cut from the length of each pant leg and replaced by a luminous band of bright red fabric. The clownish appearance this gave me was unimportant; what counted was that this outfit was actually of my size and that the jacket had a thick lining that made it luxuriously warm in comparison to the standard uniform. Now I was issued new clothes, once again the customary striped "pajamas," which were flimsier and much worse than any I had worn before. I was issued the usual blanket, metal bowl, cup, and spoon. I moved into a new barracks, with hundreds of new people. Of my friends from the old *Jugendliche* group only Artur and Miki remained. I had no idea where Willi was. (In fact, I never saw him again.)

Snapshot: It is evening in my barracks. Someone yells, "*Stillstand*" (attention). This is a signal that an SS officer had entered the barracks. Everybody immediately jumps to attention. It was important not to move, so as not to attract the attention of the passing officer. You stayed immobile until he said, "*Weitermachen*" (as you were). The officer hurries along our line. Suddenly he stops in his tracks and points at me, saying, " *Du, Junge* " (you, boy), come over here!" My knees tremble.

I can barely breathe. Being singled out like this can only mean bad news. I shuffle forward.

"Aren't you the kid who mended socks in Haselhorst ?"

"Yes," I nod my head.

"Boy, am I glad to have found you," he continues. "Since we came to Sachsenhausen I can't find anyone to mend my socks. I'll bring you some tomorrow." My terror turns to elation.

Talking to a German officer was like talking to a wrathful deity. One avoided eye contact and answered questions as succinctly as possible, without volunteering any comments. I am, however, sufficiently emboldened to point out that I will also need a needle and some yarn.

He nods his head and moves on.

The officer returned the next day with his socks, a needle, and a torn, light-blue sweater. He explained that he had not been able to obtain any yarn or thread. I was to unravel the sweater and use its wool for mending. He also instructed the *Blockälteste,* a truly nasty character, to give me a permanent space at a table and to see to it that I was not disturbed. Soon I had two balls of wool and was ready to mend the dark-gray socks with the light-blue yarn. I was back in business!

In Sachsenhausen we did not have to go to shelters during air raids. The camp was not located near any military objectives and, besides, it had no shelters large enough to hold the great number of its inmates. During the first night there, I woke up the instant I heard the siren wail. By force of habit, I moved in one smooth motion to jump off my bunk and I hit my head on the bunk above me. I realized that I was in another camp, where I did not have to get up and run to the shelters. Instantly I went back to sleep. From that night on, I never woke up when the sirens sounded. Once in a while, the sound of bombs exploding, or the shaking of our bunks from the explosions would wake me up, but I never lost much sleep over this. There was no place to hide anyway and I figured that, if we should get a direct hit, it would all be over in a flash, no matter what I did. In the meantime, sleep was precious.

When an air raid took place during the day, we were only required to stay inside the barracks. Some of us crouched under tables, on the theory that if a bomb should damage the building, the table might protect us from falling debris. I can still see myself during a daylight air raid, sitting at the table, darning socks to complete a rush job. (By this time my clientele had expanded.) The falling bombs emitted a warbling, whistling sound, from which we had learned to judge how far away the bombs were. Sometimes the whistling sound gave me the feeling that the bomb was heading straight for the top of my head. Whenever I experienced that feeling, I would slide under the table. After hearing the bomb explode, I would surface, sit up on the bench and continue my darning. Nobody could say that I was not conscientious about delivering my orders on time.

The period I am describing was April, 1945. Although the war was to end officially on May 8, we did not have any news from the outside and did not know that Russian troops had already started the great battle to capture Berlin. We deduced, however, from many signs that the end must be at hand. The air raids intensified. The prisoners who went to work outside the camp brought back tales of the fortifications the Germans were feverishly building all over Berlin. It was obvious they were preparing for the final battle. Rumors flew through the camp about what was happening, but we knew of nothing with certainty. One day an SS officer came to our *Block* and announced with a jovial air, "*Juden, euer Roosevelt ist tot.*" (Jews, your Roosevelt is dead). That is how we found out about the death of the American president. The German propaganda machine had put out that Roosevelt was a Jew, hence "your Roosevelt."

One afternoon came the announcement that the camp would be evacuated. The rumor spread that the camp would be blown up after we left and so, when the order came that all of us should take our belongings, including our blankets, and assemble on the *Appellplatz,* even those who could barely crawl, obeyed, since nobody wanted to be left behind and risk being blown up with the camp. There were about 32,000 of us who obeyed, while about 3,000 who were too sick and feeble stayed behind. The date of the start of this now infamous "Sachsenhausen Hunger March," has been established as April 20. And it turned out that the enfeebled prisoners who stayed behind were liberated by the Soviet Army on April 22.

We were divided into groups of 500. By the time the long columns of five-abreast prisoners started moving out of the camp, it was already dusk. We were forced to march for hours in the darkness. (Throughout the war, no lights were allowed to shine outdoors at night, anywhere in Germany, for fear of Allied bombardment.) SS guards and their dogs were all around us. We kept walking, even though terribly tired. I kept getting very angry with the man walking behind me because every once in a while he would poke me in my back. It took me some time to realize that I, like most of the others, was falling asleep while walking; when that happened I would slow down and the man behind me, in semi-sleep himself, would bump into me, quite unintentionally. And so we kept on walking and shuffling and bumping into one another; hearing the shouted exhortations of the guards and the barking and snarling of the dogs, and occasional sounds of rifle shots from behind.

Our group was at last herded into a barn, which had some straw on the ground, upon which we all collapsed and instantly fell asleep. We were woken up at what seemed very soon thereafter, but must have been some hours later. When we emerged from the barn we were greeted by a most incredible sight: International Red Cross trucks, painted white, with large red crosses on their sides. The trucks carried food packages. When the war was drawing to a close, Count Folke Bernadotte, a Swedish nobleman who headed the International Red Cross, decided that the organization had to help the victims of the war, even though it had not yet officially ended. Sweden had remained neutral during the War and was not attacked by Germany. So the Swedes loaded their trucks with food packages and entered the northern part of Germany and drove right across the front lines into the part still held by the Nazis. They were able to take advantage of the fact that by this time the country was in complete chaos. Wherever the Red Cross trucks encountered German army units, the Swedes explained their humanitarian mission and simply argued their way across the front lines. This mission was dangerous, without any guarantee of success, but the heroic Swedes persevered and through their action saved many prisoners during the last days of the war.

It was our good luck that some of these trucks found us on the first day of our march. The Swedes distributed their food: one carton for each four adult prisoners and one for each two juveniles. My friend Artur and I shared our first carton of food, which contained various smaller packages. The problem was that whatever we did not eat immediately was awkward and heavy to carry. Because of our weakened condition, each of us had difficulty enough just to carry himself and his rolled up blanket. So we made a deal with a still strong, healthy guy to carry our food package in exchange for a share of its contents. You can bet that we never let this fellow out of our sight. We met the Red Cross trucks a number of times during our march and they provided us with practically all the food we received. For apart from these occasional packages, the Germans gave us only minimal and sporadic food. They usually managed to get us some coffee-like, hot liquid in the mornings, but they must have had little bread themselves, so not much was left for us.

We were now part of what became infamously known as the Hunger March. It continued for twelve days. Each night we slept at a different location. Sometimes we were put up in barns, into which we were herded like the animals that were meant to inhabit them. Often we just slept outdoors, in woods next to the road. Our exhaustion was total. Each evening we thought we would not have the strength to take one more step the next day. There were two things that kept us going. You might say that one was the carrot and the other was the stick. The carrot was our expectation that any morning might bring with it our liberation and so, our immediate goal was just to last to the end of the day. The other compelling reason was the fact that whoever was unable or unwilling to walk further was shot dead by the German guards. A powerful stick, indeed.

Every once in a while a prisoner would simply give up and collapse or just sit down at the edge of the road, in spite of the urging of his comrades. A guard would come over and stay with him. Once the entire column of prisoners had passed, the guards would prod him, and others like him, exhausted beyond caring, into the ditch beside the road and shoot him dead. At numerous times we came across small piles of dead, executed prisoners, sprawled in the ditches along the road, victims from a preceding column.

There were times when I, too, was ready to give up. Whenever I faltered, one or two stronger prisoners would come to my aid. They would support me under my arms, in spite of their own exhaustion, and we would keep on walking and I would regain some little strength, out of reserves I did not know I possessed. I developed a pain in my left knee that was much more severe than the other aches and pains that racked my entire body. The pain felt like a stab of a needle whenever I bent my knee. The only way to alleviate it was to keep the leg from bending. So I developed a way of keeping my left leg stiff and dragging it behind me as I walked, and this technique helped. (A vestige of this stabbing pain stayed with me for some twenty years and still crops up at times, whenever I put a strain on my knee.) Other people developed walking problems of many sorts. We wore boots with wooden, unbending soles and canvas tops and these boots were hardly known for their great fit. They caused me pain in the soles of my feet that I tried my best to ignore. (This is another problem that plagued me for years, until an orthopedist in the U.S. prescribed metal inlays for my shoes, which I wear to this day.) Many people developed terrible blisters, but there was nothing they could do about them.

Whenever the Red Cross workers came upon us they encountered a haggard crowd of walking skeletons, dressed in filthy, tattered striped prison uniforms, devoid of human expression. We kept quite still and quiet, for any unnecessary motion, including talking, wasted precious energy. In the evenings, after we had eaten and rested a bit, we would start talking again, quietly. When meeting prisoners we did not know, the first question was, "Where do you come from?" Everyone was searching continuously for relatives and friends.

One night I was sitting next to a prisoner who asked me this customary question. When I told him I came from Trenčín in Slovakia, he excitedly asked for my name, explaining that he came from the same town. When I identified myself, he embraced me like a long-lost friend, which indeed I was. This man was about a dozen years older than I and had known me since I was an infant. Yet he could not recognize me. When he told me he was Jan Ardo, I could not relate my memory of this man to the elderly person before me. I concluded that he must be the father of the Jan Ardo I had known. (Only when I met him again a few months later, back in Trenčín, did I realize my mistake and told him that I had taken him for his own father.)

Snapshot: A few of us are standing facing the back of a white Red Cross truck. The truck is empty, having just unloaded all of its cargo. Its rear gate is down and one of the Swedes sits on the back, feet dangling, conversing with us in German. Suddenly he says to me, "Come, hop on," patting the floor of the truck with his right hand. I look at him uncomprehendingly. "Come on," he repeats, "we'll take you with us." Some of my fellow-prisoners are starting to encourage me, "Come on, what are you waiting for?" Conflicting thoughts race through my head: if I accept his offer and hop on, my war, my entire ordeal, may be over in that instant. On the other hand, what if the Germans inspect the truck before it leaves their jurisdiction and find me in it? There is no doubt in my mind that I would wind up with a bullet through my head. Within the few seconds of time available to me, I come to a decision and shake my head lightly. The Swede shrugs his shoulders, as if to say, "Well, I did my best." The truck motor springs to life; the truck starts pulling away. The Swede and I wave to each other and I wonder, did I make the right decision?

Had this happened a couple of weeks earlier I would have accepted and taken the risk without the slightest hesitation. But at this point the end seemed so near, so palpably close, that I felt that I had to decline taking any further risks. And I needed to arrive at such a fateful decision in such a brief space of time!

One night we slept again in a wood next to the highway. I was sharing a "bed" with my friend, Artur. We put one blanket on the ground underneath us and one blanket on top of us and created our usual sort of sleeping bag for two. During the night I was woken up by a light, drizzling rain. I heard some intermittent shooting not far from us. I pulled the blanket over my head to keep the rain off my face and went back to sleep. When I woke up in the morning I discovered that all our German guards and their dogs had disappeared. This was it: the long-awaited, longed-for, dreamt-about **LIBERATION.**

I rose to my feet and looked around. A profusion of abandoned military equipment lay scattered about: hastily discarded SS uniform jackets, hats, helmets, and even a couple of disabled jeep-like vehicles. I picked up and pocketed a metal whistle, a memento I have kept to date. It has an incised inscription which reads, "Westfront 1939, Gendarme Inspector Schumacher." I don't know the fate of its original owner, but his whistle obviously survived the entire long war.

Small groups of prisoners milled about. None of us had the faintest idea where we were, what to expect, or what to do. We were actually between the collapsing German military line and the advancing American army. My four friends and I quickly decided on our priorities: number one — food. We discovered a potato field nearby and immediately set to work, digging up a large pile of lovely new potatoes. We ripped a jump seat out of a burned-out German army vehicle and stripped it of its upholstery. From the metal frame we fashioned our "fireplace." One of us made a fortuitous find of a box of matches in a pocket of a discarded German uniform jacket. We found a large metal milk can, which we filled with our new potatoes and water from a nearby stream. This was placed on our "grill" and we gathered expectantly around our fire, put out our blankets and some of our clothing to dry, and waited for the potatoes to cook. Each of us also picked up a German army helmet, a number of which were lying around, ripped out its inside leather webbing, and now had a capacious bowl for our freshly boiled potatoes.

Snapshot: Five of us are sitting in a circle around our fire and our large pail. Nobody utters a word. Each of us is absolutely concentrated on his task: peeling potatoes, eating potatoes, refilling his helmet with more potatoes, EATING and EATING. We think we will never have our fill of this delicious food, but eventually, one by one, each of us is fully sated. Then we just sit there, immobile, grinning foolishly at one another, not believing that we no longer crave more food.

This feast took place on the second of May, 1945, in a place a few kilometers south of Schwerin, a town in northern Germany. It was assuredly the most memorable meal of my life.

* * *

The nucleus of this chapter was written in 1982–1983 as a memoir for my daughters. It was expanded by a number of additional details over the succeeding years.

PETER KUBICEK

Epilogue

After filling our stomachs, we wondered what to do next. We started walking slowly along the highway, looking for a town, for some authority in charge, but we saw only other ex-prisoners milling about. Suddenly, up ahead, two soldiers came into view. They were dressed in unfamiliar uniforms and wore unusual helmets. They had rifles slung casually over their shoulders and each walked on a different side of the road, eyes trained on the ditch on his side. When they came closer, we also noticed that they were chewing gum. That clinched it: they had to be American, for everyone knew from pre-war movies that Americans chewed gum. I had studied English before the war and now I ran toward them and asked them excitedly, in English, "Are you Americans ?" "Yeah," was the laconic reply. I started explaining in my rudimentary English that we were liberated prisoners and asked them what they suggested we do. One of them jerked his thumb in the direction they had come and said, "Just keep going until you hit the town. They'll take care of you there."

My first two Americans showed no surprise whatever at seeing an emaciated kid in a dirty prison uniform, who was speaking to them in English. They continued walking leisurely, concentrating their attention on the ditches. At a later date I told this story to another American soldier and wondered what those soldiers had been looking for. He laughed and said, "Souvenirs."

Here was the spearhead of the American army, entering enemy territory, and they were looking for war souvenirs.

After walking a couple of miles, we came to the town of Schwerin. It was a beehive of activity: ex-prisoners and American soldiers were swarming about. The Americans directed us toward a former German army compound for food and lodging. As we passed a town park, I came across some of Willi's "green-triangle" friends. They hailed me and we asked each other whether anyone had seen Willi. No one of us had seen him. They busied themselves setting up a campsite in the park and cooking. They invited me and my friends Miki and Artur to stay with them. Artur declined and decided to go on, but to Miki and me the prospect of an army compound had the odor of a concentration camp about it, and so we gladly accepted the invitation.

So, how did Artur and I part? We had been together through so much: in Heinkel, sleeping on the concrete floor, we used our breath and bodies to warm each other; we were together in all the *Jugendliche* groups of the camps that followed; we shared our first Red Cross food package; we shared our "bed" on the forest ground of the last night of the Hunger March; and we had recently shared our first meal of freedom.

So, here is the question: what did we say to each other? And here is the answer: nothing. He left — I stayed.

We were not callous; we were not insensitive. We were simply emotionally dead. In all the previous months, Artur and I had communicated only as much as was necessary for our survival. We knew nothing about each other's previous life ... where we came from ... any details about our families ... I never even knew his last name, nor did he know mine. Artur and Miki were somehow not real people to me: they were part of my concentration camp experience and thus, by definition, surreal. Everybody I met during this experience remained surreal to me, with the notable exception of my childhood friend Franzo, who represented my previous, hence my real, life and who had been a bridge to the childhood I had lost. He was the only one with whom I was able to communicate beyond my immediate basic needs.

Artur and I parted and we never saw each other again.

Our fragile emotional state was one that all survivors shared and there was nobody "from the outside" who gave the least bit of thought to our deep psychic problems. Taking care of our physical needs was a daunting enough task; terms such as "post-traumatic stress syndrome" or "grief management" had not even been invented. Ultimately, each of us had to find his or her own path of return to normalcy, an often circuitous road, strewn with obstacles. Some of us made it back better than others, but each survivor was left with his private emotional scars.

A number of ex-prisoner campsites were sprinkled throughout the park. Later, a couple of American army trucks came along and the soldiers started throwing down and distributing a variety of foodstuffs and clothing. We all happily grabbed whatever we could.

Our first night of freedom was similar to our last night of captivity in that we once again slept on the ground, wrapped in our concentration camp blankets. Our mood, though, was ebullient: we were gay, full of chatter and laughter; the ground seemed soft and fragrant.

The following morning, Miki and I decided to go into the center of town and see what it looked like. We soon found the town's principal street. There we walked amid German natives who were ogling the two kids in prisoner uniforms. No one spoke to us. After a few blocks, two American M.P's stopped us. These military policemen were instantly recognizable by the large "MP" stenciled on their helmets and their MP armband insignia. One was a huge man and the other was short and stocky. The smaller one addressed us in what sounded like Yiddish.

Yiddish was not spoken where I grew up. I first heard it in the concentration camps and I was able to understand much of it from my knowledge of German. Yiddish acquires words and inflections of the language of the country where it is spoken. This soldier spoke American Yiddish and odder still, it was Yiddish with the strangest twang. It was in any case a language unlike any I had ever heard. It was only later that I learned that my first friendly American came from Austin, Texas. I explained to him that I understood some English and told him if he would just speak it slowly I would understand him better. After chatting a bit, the soldiers directed us to an address where, they told us, we would find other Jewish young people. They told us to say who had sent us and assured us that we would be welcomed there. We followed their directions and soon entered the best residential part of town. At the given address was a large house -- actually two adjoining villas. In it we found about twenty Jewish girls, all in their twenties, and a few Jewish boys, all of them ex-prisoners.

We had been directed to a private enterprise of a small group of American Jewish GI's. They had appropriated these two houses and created a haven for young Jews. Every day they brought us food, clothing and their warm friendship. Individual soldiers dropped in throughout the day; in the evenings they all came to spend time with us. They listened to incredible tales of the Holocaust, related in a Babel of tongues. One of these soldiers brought me a new suit and complete change of clothes. I happily discarded all my dirty prison clothes and consigned them to the garbage.

To our surprise, most of the girls were from Slovakia. All of them had been deported to Auschwitz in 1942 and had survived three years of concentration camps. When the first transports of unmarried young people came from Slovakia to Auschwitz, the men's section of the camp had already been organized. Poles had already taken the better camp jobs. The young women from Slovakia, however, were the first ones in the new women's camp of Birkenau. Many of them became the first *Prominente* of this section. As a result, more Slovak women than men survived the hell of Auschwitz. These girls whom I now met all appeared well fed and decently dressed. What's more, they all had hair, a sure sign of their higher camp status, while all other women ex-prisoners were identifiable by their shaved heads. It boggled my mind that all these pleasant, chattering young women had survived an incredible three years of concentration camps. They eagerly took care of me and my friend Miki and it soon seemed to us as if we had suddenly acquired twenty mothers. This had its pros and cons. It was truly luxurious to be cared for, but to be told what to do and what not to do did not sit well with me. At this point, submitting to any authority was about the last thing I was willing to accept. However, after some tug-of-war, we established a *modus vivendi* and I formed alliances with some of the girls I liked, those who were not too bossy.

The very first evening in this new haven, I met all our American protectors, including one who came from New York City. I excitedly told him that my father lived in New York and asked him to please write to him and tell him that he had met me. I could not understand his seeming reluctance to do so and, as we spoke, I noticed that he had this baffled look on his face. It took me a while to realize that he just did not believe me and did not quite know what to say to me. With some desperation, I told him, "Look, my father's name is Andrew Kubiček and he lives at 789 West End Avenue, in New York City. Please write him, just write him a short letter." He finally promised to do so.

What he actually did was to write to his sister who lived in the Bronx and told her that he had come across this Jewish kid who claimed he had a father living in New York, which seemed such an unlikely story. He asked her to find out whether there was in fact an Andrew Kubicek, and, if so, to tell him that his son was alive and well. Upon receipt of that letter, his sister opened the Manhattan telephone directory and found my father listed, at the precise address I had given.

She phoned my father at his apartment — actually a furnished room — during the day, while he was at work. His landlady was in the room, cleaning it, and answered the call and gave the caller my father's office number. That is how my father received the news of my survival. He asked some questions, but was so overcome by emotion that his hands shook and he was unable to write. He asked his secretary to get on the telephone extension and to write down everything that was said. It was the first time in three years that he had news about me.

My father habitually carried a pocket diary with him, in which he entered his appointments and major events of his days. I have kept his diaries from 1945 and 1946. Here is his entry, in the tiny handwriting he used for this purpose, for May 25, 1945:

> *Received message from Mrs. Kurt Elias, of 615 West 173 Street, that her brother, Pfc. Herbert Saalfeld, found Peter in camp in Germany, in good health. No news about Ilka [my mother]. Sent cable, letter and package to Pfc. Saalfeld.*

I do not know how long this exchange of letters took. In those days, letters from Europe to the U.S. took quite a few days. And letters from the U.S. to military personnel had to be addressed to a U.S. Army address and from there were distributed further. This was quite a time-consuming process. By the time Herbert Saalfeld received my father's cable a number of weeks had passed and by that time I was no longer in Schwerin. The Army had developed a system for dealing with the mass of ex-prisoners and displaced people. All the ex-prisoners in northern Germany were moved to the town of Lübeck, a northern seaport. There we were housed in German army barracks, since that was the only sensible way of accommodating all of us. I was now living in a dormitory room furnished with double-decker bunks, together with my friend Miki and the Slovak girls. The rest of the compound was home to ex-prisoners from Czechoslovakia, Hungary, Yugoslavia, and Russia.

There was an open central court between the barracks where we could walk around and socialize with these polyglot groups of ex-prisoners. Lots of fascinating personal stories were exchanged. One day I came upon a band concert in progress which some of the men had organized. It had attracted a large group of listeners. The musicians were standing in a semicircle, with their leader/conductor in the center. And who was leading this band? None other than my friend Janos, the Hungarian gypsy violinist who had played so memorably at the Camp Inak Christmas party. I was certainly glad to see that he had made it and, as I moved closer to him, his face broke out in a big smile of recognition, without missing a beat in his performance.

The army captain in charge of our camp took a liking to me. He presented me with some additional clothes, a raincoat and shoes. Seeing my severely emaciated condition, he also arranged for me to be examined at a local German hospital. I spent two days and one night there and was given a thorough examination by the German physicians. At first they refused to believe me that I was fifteen years old, estimating that I could at most be twelve. I was already getting used to this common reaction. In this hospital, for the first time since my liberation, I came into direct contact with Germans: the other patients and the hospital staff. As soon as they found out my background, to a man they volunteered the assurance that they were not Nazis.

> **Snapshot:** A beautiful, sunny May day. I am between appointments for medical exams and decide to step outside for some fresh air. I am inside a hospital courtyard. Several ambulatory German patients are also here, taking in the sun. One of them starts talking to me. Realizing quickly that I do not speak like a native, he asks me where I come from. I tell him.

"So, how come you are here ?" he asks.

"I was recently liberated from a concentration camp.

"Really! *Was hast du ausgefressen?*" This is a German slang expression which literally means, "What did you guzzle up or devour?" It implies, "What kind of crime did you commit?"

"Well, my crime is that I am a Jew."

There is a moment of silence.

"*Ach*, those Nazis!" he says then. "You know, I was never a Nazi," he continues.

Some of the other men, who had overheard us, now come over and volunteer the information that they, too, were never Nazis. I quickly hear that none of them had ever been a Nazi, had never met a Nazi; had, in fact, never even known a single Nazi.

The day the war ended, it appears that, in a single puff of smoke, all Nazis magically disappeared.

By this extension, since all German war crimes were committed exclusively by the Nazis, once the latter disappeared, only "us good Germans" remained. This may have been a comforting thought to the Germans, but it was, and remains, nothing but a myth. Millions of Germans clung to the belief that just a small clique of criminals bore sole responsibility for the Holocaust. The fact is that a great many ordinary Germans, soldiers, policemen, and various other groups of citizens were involved in perpetrating atrocities.

And from there it was but a small further step to the myth of, "We didn't even know." And the world promptly swallowed this fake propaganda. From then on, through the present, we hear only about Nazi crimes in connection with the War, as in "Nazi murderers, Nazi soldiers." The fact is that there never was such a concept as a Nazi soldier. The German Wehrmacht was composed of a highly professional military cadre, as well as of volunteers, such as the S.S. and, of course, ordinary German conscripts. On many later occasions, when I described our torturers as Germans, I was asked whether I did not mean the Nazis. My answer is, "Well, some of them may have been Nazis — I don't really know — but what I do know for sure is that they were Germans." Whenever we saw their dreaded uniforms we knew we faced Germans, all of whom represented utmost danger and that's how we viewed them. And, incidentally, the Germans did not view American soldiers as the "Democratic Army" either: it was the Germans against the Americans, or against the Red Army.

On the second day the doctors gave me their diagnosis: I suffered from severe malnutrition (hardly news to me) and most probably tuberculosis. The latter shocked and depressed me. Upon being discharged, I went for a long walk in some nearby fields. I felt very alone and very sorry for myself. I had no news of my mother, or my father, and now I was just given the news of my dreadful illness. Slowly I made my way back to our compound.

There I came upon a merry scene. Herbert Saalfeld and two of our other GI friends from Schwerin had come to visit us. They had brought some food and drink and a reunion party was in progress. When Saalfeld received my father's cable, and proof that the story I had told him was true, he must have felt a little guilty and decided to drive to Lübeck to see me and to bring me my father's cable. After tears of sorrow during my walk in the fields, I now shed tears of utter joy.

PETER KUBICEK

My Mother's Story

My mother stayed in Bergen-Belsen throughout her internment. This was a huge camp, with many divisions and sub-divisions, in which conditions varied from sub-human to infernal. Its population kept growing and growing. In the latter part of 1944 and early 1945, as the Russian army kept pressing forward from the East, the Germans kept shutting down the extermination camps in Poland. In their final frenzy to make Europe *Judenrein* (clean of Jews), the Germans kept deporting the remnants of Jewry to Germany, rather than to Poland. Many of these deportees wound up in Bergen-Belsen. When Auschwitz was liquidated in January, 1945, its remaining prisoners were also transferred to Bergen-Belsen. Estimates vary, but the total population of this camp may have swelled to 100,000.

Its barracks were insufficient for so large a population. Conditions were indescribable. When latrine facilities became inadequate, the Germans had prisoners dig trenches right alongside the barracks to serve as latrines. Diseases were rampant. Dysentery was just one of these. Typhus was another. The starved prisoners had little resistance to disease. Every injury, every little scratch one got could develop into a tragedy since our starved bodies just did not heal. An open wound, coupled with the lack of hygiene, could fester and just refuse to heal, and become increasingly worse. In addition to wounds, people developed all kinds of sores, scabs, pussy boils.

My mother had always had poor circulation in her legs. In the 1930's she developed problems along her shinbones. X-rays were the treatment of the time and these caused her condition more harm than good and actually burned her skin. In Bergen-Belsen she developed large wounds on her legs, which refused to heal, and got steadily worse. (She was to suffer from this condition for the rest of her life.) My mother became a fanatic about cleanliness while in the camp, believing that as long as she kept herself clean she could avoid the widespread diseases. It is impossible to imagine the effort cleanliness required. Most people simply did not have the energy for it and just let themselves go.

The death toll in Bergen-Belsen was staggering. As barracks emptied of life, they were used to warehouse corpses. Instead of burying them, prisoners were ordered to stack them in neat rows, head to toe, and layer upon layer. The bodies were just left that way to putrefy. When spotted typhus broke out, almost nobody escaped this highly contagious disease.

Toward the middle of April, my mother succumbed to typhus. She remembered only becoming feverish and laying lifeless and delirious on her bunk. Her luck was that Bergen-Belsen was liberated by British and Canadian troops on April 15. My mother told me later that when she came to she found herself in a bed with clean white sheets. Looking around she saw other white beds, as well as white-uniformed nurses, conversing quietly. At that instant she believed that she had died and had gone to heaven. In fact, she was in a British field hospital.

The British troops had an overwhelming job in Bergen-Belsen. Thousands of bodies were strewn in piles. Thousands of prisoners were deathly ill. Some 30,000 prisoners died within the first few weeks after liberation. The British coped heroically. They conscripted captured German soldiers and civilians to help with the clean-up and the burial of the bodies. They brought in medical personnel to take care of the sick. Their organization certainly saved my mother's life.

The British now compiled lists of the surviving prisoners and circulated them throughout the other refugee camps in Germany. Survivors searching for their family members pored over them eagerly. These lists even came to the U.S., where my father read them. This is the succinct entry from his pocket diary, for June 1, 1945.

> *Ilka listed in Block 56 Hospital, camp Belsen-Bergen [sic], in Bulletin of World Jewish Congress. Sent cable to Fred [my mother's brother in England] and to Pfc. Herbert Saalfeld.*

While recuperating in the hospital my mother found the following listing in one of these bulletins:

Peter Kubiček, from Trenčín, Czechoslovakia, survivor of Auschwitz, currently in Lübeck.

The mistaken Auschwitz label was due to my being with the group of Auschwitz girls. My mother was convinced that this could only be me. As soon as she could, she checked herself out of the hospital and, walking on heavily bandaged legs, went to see the British area commander. She showed him my name on the list and asked him to help her find me. The commander told her that he had his hands full with the problems of Bergen-Belsen and tried to reassure her that she could look forward to a reunion with me as soon as we were both repatriated. That was not good enough for my mother and she persisted.

"Do you have children ?" she asked him.

"Yes," he allowed.

"Well, how would you feel if your child had been torn from you and sent to a terrifying, unknown fate, with the chance that you would never see him again? Once you found out he was alive, would you not want to see him immediately?"

"Well, what do you want me to do, woman?" burst out the commander. "Get you a car and a military escort to chase all over Germany to find him?"

"Yes, that is precisely what I want you to do!" rejoined my mother.

The commander fell silent. "Come back tomorrow," he said finally. "I'll see what I can do."

The next day, when my mother appeared in his office, the commander picked up the phone and ordered a soldier to come in.

"Here is a requisition for a car," he said to him. "Drive this woman to Lübeck and help her find her son."

When my mother arrived in our camp in Lübeck, she caused a sensation. The sudden appearance of a survivor's relative was alike to seeing someone rise from the dead. Only I was no longer there.

Reunion

As soon as the American army organized transports to repatriate survivors, Miki and I, as two of the youngest, were assigned to the very first group. Our transport consisted of two open trucks, with benches along each side. As our truck crossed Germany, we marveled at the devastation we saw. Lübeck, although a port, was situated several miles inland, and even though the port had been heavily bombed, the town itself was pretty much unscathed. But once we left Lübeck, we passed through other towns that were totally bombed out and ruined. The last major German city we passed through was Dresden. The annihilation there seemed total. Our trucks made their way through rubble bulldozed to the sides of the roadway. I did not see one single habitable building.

We crossed into Czechoslovakia and finally arrived at our destination, Prague. The trucks with returning survivors all continued to a particular central town square. Along the way, cheers and applause from the population accompanied us. A large crowd gathered on that square every day. Many people awaited the trucks, hoping to find family members, or obtain news about anyone they had known. As soon as we jumped off the truck, we were surrounded by a throng of people asking questions: In which camp have you been?… Where do you come from?… Did you know so-and-so?… The questions were endless and we volunteered our answers and our stories. At times, extraordinary, emotional scenes occurred, when long-separated relatives found each other, to a great flow of tears and applause and additional tears from bystanders.

Our group was finally led to a YWCA, where we received rooms and were promised three meals a day. Each of us also received a small amount of pocket money and a pass for free rides on all public transportation. The next few days we joined the throngs at the square of the returning transports, where we waited for arriving trucks and talked with some of the many people waiting there. I had the great satisfaction of meeting a man whom I could tell that his sister was among the group of Auschwitz girls I had met in Germany.

I was desperately seeking news of my mother. Some trucks finally arrived from Bergen-Belsen and on one of them I recognized Mrs. Eckstein. She and her son had been with us on the transport to Bergen-Belsen; her son had been in my group of *Jugendliche* in Inak and Haselhorst. I was happy to tell her that her son and I had been together for most of the time and that she would no doubt see him soon. And she confirmed that my mother was alive. At first I had some difficulty communicating with this woman. She seemed unable to hear me properly and was unsteady on her feet. My mother later told me that Mrs. Eckstein had been badly beaten by an SS guard who caught her taking a piece of wood from a construction site. He had knocked her to the ground and kicked her head repeatedly. As a result, she had lost most of her hearing and it had affected her balance.

I kept up my vigil for the truck transports. One day, Miki and I were just returning from lunch when we spotted two trucks on their way to the square with our group of Slovak girls on board. We scrambled up onto one of the trucks for a grand reunion with our friends. And they told me about my mother's miraculous appearance in Lübeck. I was now even more anxious to be reunited with her.

Snapshot: I am standing in line on the street in front of the YWCA, waiting to go in for lunch. The street slopes somewhat downhill. I look back towards the end of the line and see a woman talking to some people. She has close-cropped hair and is painfully thin, yet there is something awfully familiar about her. I take a few steps downhill. I feel my throat constricting as my heart leaps up into it — it is my mother! We bound into each other's arms, clinging to each other and trying to keep our balance on the sloping sidewalk. Our sobs and tears of joy seem never-ending.

1945-1946: The Aftermath

The liberated survivors returned to their native towns with mixed feelings. Entire Jewish communities had been wiped out and had simply disappeared. Everyone's assumption was that his family, relatives and friends were all dead. Upon encountering someone familiar, our reaction was, "You are alive ? How wonderful !" We, like most survivors found our family possessions gone. Former Jewish apartments were occupied by new inhabitants who did not look upon the returnees with great favor. When my mother and I came back to Trenčín we found with joy that our friend Ilush Polak, my mother's wartime business partner, and her husband were alive. They and the group of Jewish doctors who had worked and lived in the hospital all remained protected in this haven. The Polaks still had their old as well as their hospital apartments and they generously offered their town apartment to us.

When the persecution of Jews started, many people asked gentile acquaintances to hide some of their possessions. This was generally readily agreed to and suitcases of silverware, linens, better dishes and other possessions of value were smuggled into non-Jewish houses. Once the Jewish owners were deported, their suitcases were invariably opened, examined and their possessions absorbed into the households. Some Jews had now returned and asked for their possessions back. These requests were generally met with the claim that everything was gone. The most common excuse was, *"Rusi zobrali."* (The Russians took it.) The Russian army did its share of looting and they became convenient scapegoats, even in places where they had never set foot. The common plaint of the Slovaks was, "Of all the Jews who were deported, just mine has to return!" Oh, the unfairness of life! Most survivors did not have the strength to argue and were still too suspicious of the authorities to turn to them for help.

My mother had left some of our possessions with Mrs. Kubinska, the woman who hid us for the few weeks before we were caught, and who had been well paid for her efforts. She now refused to give anything back to us, using the familiar *"Rusi zobrali"* excuse. My mother was not so easily put off and took her case to the police. During a confrontation with Mrs. Kubinska at the police station, my mother noticed a very familiar handkerchief sticking out of the woman's breast pocket. "If you will examine the handkerchief that Mrs. Kubinska is wearing," said my mother to a policeman, "you will find that it has my initials on it." My mother got most of her possessions back.

Next my mother turned her attention to Mr. Masnik, the man who had "aryanized" our living room furniture four years earlier. She rang his doorbell, accompanied by a burly friend. The man opened the door and became pretty nervous when he recognized my mother. The *"Rusi zobrali"* excuse was obviously not going to work, as our furniture was right there in his living room. My mother told him that all she wanted back were her Persian rugs and the content of one display cabinet in which she had a small collection of antique objects, including some Judaica. This was there intact, exactly the way my mother had showcased it. She opened the sliding glass doors and took out the objects. She then produced a screwdriver and proceeded to unscrew the shelf that had supported the objects. Underneath was a second, concealed shelf, which a cabinetmaker friend had devised for us. This secret shelf held all my mother's jewelry. There it was, well protected and undisturbed these past four years. I only wish

I had been present and could have seen the expression on the man's face as he watched my mother scoop up her jewelry!

My problem at this time was my precarious health. Soon after we came back to Trenčín I developed pleurisy. I spent some time in the hospital and my pleura had to be drained of the fluid that kept pooling there. I had a constant low-grade fever, a symptom of tuberculosis. At that time the only treatment available for this disease was bed rest, so that the lungs be used as little as possible and be allowed to heal by themselves. Breathing good, clean mountain air was considered beneficial and I was advised to enter a TB sanatorium. There were a number of these in the High Tatra Mountains of Slovakia. The one I was sent to was a former hotel, with spartan, but comfortable accommodations. Each patient had his own private room with bathroom and balcony. Mornings I was woken up when breakfast on a tray was brought to my room and then I would lie on a chaise on the balcony and allow the clear mountain air confer its benefits upon my lungs. When the weather was cool, a nurse's aide came and tucked me into a blanket. Lunch was served in the dining room and was followed by another few hours of rest on the balcony. In the late afternoon, most of us were permitted a short walk outdoors, and dinner followed soon thereafter. After dinner we were allowed a short period of socializing in the lounge and then it was early to bed.

A number of patients were concentration camp survivors. We tended to stick together. We split into two categories: those who unequivocally refused to talk about their experiences — the majority, including myself — and those who recounted them endlessly. From the latter I obtained a huge fund of stories, some of which defied belief. Everyone's story of survival was unique. Here I came upon a man who told me that he, too, had been in Sachsenhausen. I eagerly tried to compare notes with him, to find out whether we may have been together at one time. He just laughed and assured me that there was no way our paths could have crossed. He then told me a story that I first thought too fantastic to be true, but which turned out to be entirely accurate and I became totally riveted by it.

My new friend was part of a *Kommando* which was sequestered in a special part of the camp that was so secret that it was not even known to the ordinary SS guards, while we ordinary prisoners certainly knew nothing about it. There my friend was housed in a *Block* that contained individual beds, as distinct from the customary three-tiered wooden bunks; featuring the unheard-of luxury of sheets and pillows; individual private lockers; the *Block* was heated and it had its own bathrooms and toilets. Its inmates were better clothed and, above all, better fed. After work they enjoyed playing ping-pong, and in the evenings they played cards, chess, they sang, they told jokes. They even produced their own cabaret whose performances were attended by the SS officers. They were totally isolated from the camp's other prisoners and, importantly, did not even have to take part in the dreaded routine of the daily *Appell*.

All this was possible because of the unique work they performed: the counterfeiting of British paper currency, mainly five-pound notes. For this super-secret operation, the Germans combed the concentration camps and assembled a large team of some 140 counterfeiters: prisoners with special skills such as printers, typographers, engravers, graphic artists, forgers. My friend had been a professional photographer and had been picked for this skill. Within the SS command that initiated this scheme, it was code-named Operation Bernhard, for the man who ran it, SS Major Bernhard Krueger. He realized that these highly skilled workers were not expendable and that in order to get them to use their intellect and dexterity to achieve his objective, he had to first transform them from their semi-savage state into human beings, by giving them an atmosphere that resembled life. They in turn worked with the knowledge that their privileged status depended on their performance and on attaining the set goal, no matter how elusive it seemed. After a lot of trial and error, this operation ultimately became the greatest and most successful counterfeit scheme in history. The British banknotes they eventually printed were distributed and used throughout occupied Europe and even in neutral countries such as Switzerland and Turkey. They became a major headache for banks and particularly for the Bank of England which struggled with the problem of these fakes for some years beyond the war, ultimately discarding all their five-pound notes and replacing them with a new design. These counterfeits are considered to be among the most perfect ever produced. One of the original printing presses used is still on view today at the Sachsenhausen Memorial Museum. In 2007, a movie based on this operation was released under the title *The Counterfeiters* and won the Oscar for Best Foreign Language Film.

I spent most of my time reading English books and magazines that my father sent me and writing him letters, also in English. All in all, it was an extremely peaceful existence, undisturbed by any outside events. My main concerns were, how long would it take before I could join my father in America; before I would regain my health; and how long before I would get free of my periodic nightmares. In common with most survivors, my nights were regularly disturbed by a private nightmare, which kept recurring with only minor variations:

I am running down some dark streets. There is no one about, but "they" are after me. I hear their angry shouts behind me, all in harsh, guttural German. They come closer and closer. My terror increases. I run ever faster, this way and that, but keep running into dead-ends. I am unable to find a way out. The dream concludes abruptly upon my waking up in a sweat. It takes me a while to realize where I am and that I am safe. My breathing and pulse gradually return to normal.

This may not have been the best thing for my lungs, which were supposed to stay as evenly quiet as possible. As time passed, the nightmares fortunately diminished in frequency, if not in intensity. It took me several years to be rid of them.

The day my father learned I was alive, he began energetically trying to obtain permission for me, and then for my mother, to immigrate to the U.S. Even though by this time my father was a U.S. citizen, and we were his closest family, it was no easy matter to obtain our visas. It was a pattern that held true for most countries: they were willing to give material assistance to the survivors, but their doors were firmly shut to immigrants. Many survivors remained in Germany, unwilling to risk going back to their former homelands where nothing but desolation awaited them. They stayed instead in D.P. (Displaced Persons) camps that the Allies maintained. Many survivors who did return to their homelands, discouraged and disillusioned there, came back to Germany to the D.P. camps. Numerous marriages took place there and babies were born. All the while these survivors tried to obtain permission to immigrate to other countries. This was a very slow and difficult process since most countries of the world wanted to have nothing to do with the survivors.

Immediately after the war, the only country that opened its doors was Sweden. They did so at the urging of Count Bernadotte, a member of the Swedish royal family and the head of the heroic International Red Cross. Not only did Sweden take in survivors, but they took in the sickest and feeblest. Many of these had to be nursed for years until they regained their health. The Swedes did so and allowed them to stay in their country if they wished. My childhood friend, Franzo Goldner, was one of them. He was liberated in Bergen-Belsen and then had the horrifying experience of having to watch his father die in his arms. He was told by the Swedes that unless he allowed them to give him better care, in Sweden, his chances of survival were no better than his father's. He ultimately married a fellow survivor, became a Swedish citizen and brought up two wonderful daughters, Suzanne and Katrin, who take such devoted care of him in his old age.

Many survivors tried to go to Palestine. This land, however, was controlled by the British, who were opposed to Jewish immigration. Many tried to get there anyway, illegally, and, when caught by the British, were deported to D.P. camps in Cyprus. It was not until 1948, when the State of Israel was established, that many survivors were able to leave the D.P. camps of Germany and Cyprus.

PETER KUBICEK

A Very Brief List: Relatives Who Survived

My mother had one brother, Fred, who was two years her junior. When the war started, he was living in Paris. A convinced Francophile, he had great faith in the French army. He found soon out that his faith was misplaced. He also soon found himself "drafted as a volunteer" in the Czechoslovak army in exile. The Czechs used this phrase without irony and ignored its oxymoronic connotation. As the German army threatened Paris, the Czechs embarked upon the military maneuver at which they historically excelled — they ordered a retreat. Their goal was to reach the southern French port of Marseilles, where the British had promised to pick them up by ship.

My uncle Fred owned a car before the war and was very familiar with France's highways. When his army superiors learned of his experience they made him the driver of the lead truck of the convoy transporting the army south. He led them unerringly to Marseilles, where the British ships were indeed waiting. After the troops descended from the trucks, Fred was ordered to lead the convoy of empty trucks back to Paris. Instead he led them a few miles away to an isolated stretch of beach, where they abandoned the vehicles and then made their way onto the British ships. There Fred quickly made himself useful to the British military as he was one of the few Czechs who spoke English. This did not increase his popularity among the Czech officers. He told the story of the time he and a few English-speaking young

Czech Jewish men stood on board, conversing with the British. A couple of Czech officers stood nearby and he overheard one of them say in Czech, "Just look at those Jews — right away they speak English." Shades of my it's-easy-for-him-he's-a-Jew story! As soon as he reached England, Fred volunteered for the British army, where he served throughout the war. He settled in England, where he spent the rest of his life and ultimately became a very successful hotel owner. When he died he was managing director of Grand Metropolitan Hotels, a company he helped found, which had become one of the largest in the world.

My mother's parents came from very large families. She had innumerable aunts, uncles and cousins. Whenever I visited my grandparents in Miroslav I could never keep track of all the relatives who welcomed me. My mother remained on very close terms with many of her cousins. Of all of these, only three male cousins survived the war.

Hugo Horner, with his wife Grete and son Tommy, was the only one prescient enough to emigrate before the war to Palestine. There his son changed his name to Eli and after his schooling became one of the founders of Kibbutz Saar. I visited him there once in the 1950's and he took me hiking all over Israel. He married in the kibbutz and had two children. During the Israeli war with Lebanon he was shot and killed when the Hezbollah ambushed the bus he was riding.

Ernst Horner survived Theresienstadt and Auschwitz, while his wife and child were gassed as soon as they arrived in Auschwitz. After the war he married a fellow survivor whom he had met in Theresienstadt, whose husband had been exterminated. They immigrated to Australia where Ernst ran a successful lumber business.

Hans Bader was my mother's youngest cousin. He was 10 years younger than she. My mother knew him since birth and loved him. She liked to help her aunt care for him and carried him around, played with him, took him to visit other relatives.

In 1942, Hansi, as my mother called him, was deported with his mother to Theresienstadt. He was 28 years old.

In Theresienstadt, in the midst of all the misery, he fell in love with a girl named Inge and they insisted on getting married, in spite of their uncertain future. How and even whether the marriage was consummated I do not know, since unmarried men and women were accommodated in separate houses, at opposite ends of the ghetto. However, Hansi and Inge wanted to affirm their love and devotion to each other through a formal marriage and so that's what they did: "... till death do us part," indeed!

They and their mothers did not escape deportation to Auschwitz. In late 1944, when the Germans, under pressure from the Russian army from the east, started to liquidate their extermination camps in Poland, Hans wound up in Bergen-Belsen, the same camp in which my mother was. After liberation, he, too, found himself in a British field hospital, suffering from typhus and a dangerously gangrenous leg. One day they brought him the news that one Inge Bader was found in Bergen-Belsen. He immediately asked to see her, but both he and she were too weak to get up and out of their beds. After a few weeks, when he was allowed to start walking on crutches, he requested to be taken to see Inge. He was carried to another building and deposited in front of a room. He hobbled inside, with the aid of a nurse. There he faced three beds, each occupied by an immobile, skeletal human being. Only their small, shaven skulls were exposed. He threw a desperate look toward the nurse and she understood that he could not tell which one was his wife. She led him to one bed and said gently, "This is Inge Bader." He still could not recognize his 25-year old wife. She, however, recognized him. Incapable of talking, she only cried silently and held his hand. Ultimately, they were both taken to Sweden, where he was gradually nursed back to health, but she was so weakened that she succumbed to her illness and died. Hans made a new life in Sweden, marrying again, bringing up a son, Stefan, and living to a ripe old age.

Of my father's numerous relatives, only two survived: his niece Eva Füredi and cousin Kornel Marton. Eva, after surviving Auschwitz, emigrated to Palestine, where she married, had a son, Arieh, and became grandmother to three girls. Kornel, my bachelor uncle, survived in hiding. He, alone of both sides of my family, stayed in Slovakia after the war, married, and had a son, Palko, and ultimately two grandsons.

Final Statistics

Population of Slovak Jews at the beginning of 1942: 89,500

Deported in 1942: 59,500

Deported in 1944: 10,500

Total deported: 70,000

Of the 70,000 deportees fewer than 4,000 survived. Jewish population of my hometown of Trenčín at the beginning of 1942: about 2,000

Of these, about 425 survived.

Of my Jewish elementary class of about 30 children of my age, three girls and I survived.

Of the class above me, two girls and three boys survived.

Only one of my classmates remained in Trenčín after the war.

Three who survived: myself, Franzo Goldner, and Paul Strassmann, on a hike in 1940.

57 years later — in 1997 — "the boys" recreate their original pose, at Paul Strassmann's swimming pool.

And So, At Long Last...

In November, 1946, one-and-a-half years after my father applied for U.S. visas for my mother and me, they were finally granted. My father applied at the same time for a visa for Paul Strassmann, the orphaned son of my father's best friend, but it took a further two years for his visa to be granted.

With visas in hand, all we yearned for was to get to the U.S. as fast as possible. Few passenger ships, however, made the trip at the time and passage was difficult to obtain. Nor was it easy to obtain a passport. It had taken us about nine months to obtain one from the newly reconstituted, democratic republic of Czechoslovakia. A passport was not a citizen's automatic right: it was a favor granted by the state. Many countries then, and still today, believed that its citizens were here to serve the state, rather than the other way around. And since the state at the time wished to discourage post-war emigration of its citizens, it simply restricted the issuance of passports. We finally received these after numerous applications and our passports contained the following stipulation. "This passport is valid for six months, for all countries of Europe, for the USA, and not back." What a perfect illustration of the bureaucratic pettiness and small-mindedness of the country — and a perfect goodbye kiss from a country we were anxious to leave — with not a chance that we would wish to return.

So my father booked us on the new, modern way to travel, via airplane. Since commercial airline passenger service across the Atlantic did not arrive till the late thirties, and in 1939 was promptly suspended by the war, this was mode of travel still had a magic-carpet feeling to it. We left Trenčín by train and traveled some hours to Prague. There we stayed overnight with Ernest Horner, my mother's cousin, in his tiny apartment, with my mother sleeping on his living room couch and I on the living room carpet. The next morning we boarded a KLM flight from Prague to Amsterdam, where the airline put us up for the night in a hotel, a new and luxurious experience. The following day we boarded KLM flight #101, named "The Flying Dutchman," a propeller-driven Lockheed Constellation. The first leg of the flight took us from Amsterdam to Santa Maria in the Azores, islands off the coast of Portugal. There we deplaned and had dinner, to us a most elegant meal, while the plane was refueled and the crew changed. We next flew from Santa Maria to Gander airport in Sidney, Newfoundland. There we deplaned for breakfast while another refueling took place. The last leg was from Newfoundland to New York, our promised land.

Final snapshot: My mother and I are walking on a ramp that leads to the arrival lounge of the Marine Air Terminal at LaGuardia Airport. Above us, on the roof of the terminal, is an observation deck where friends of arriving passengers are waiting, ranged along a railing. Suddenly, we hear a voice from this terrace above calling, "Ilka, Ilka…"

I look up and see my father at the railing, furiously waving his arms. We are unable to wave back since we are both carrying hand luggage. Then my father calls out, "Where is Peter?" I am walking right alongside my mother, but my father is looking for the nine-year old boy he remembers from seven years ago, and he does not recognize me. I put down my luggage and wave to my father.

The date is November 13, 1946. My new life begins.

One year after my arrival in the U.S., in front of our house on Booth Street, in Forest Hills. Having been forced to spend the previous year confined to my bed, to further my recuperation from tuberculosis, I had by this time reached the weight of 136 lbs. This was more than double my weight upon my liberation and the heaviest I have ever been.

Peter Kubicek in his current role as a docent at The Metropolitan Museum of Art in New York City, lecturing in front of Jackson Pollock's seminal modern painting *Autumn Rhythm*.